MODERN LOVE

Revised and Updated

MODERN LOVE

Revised and Updated

TRUE STORIES OF LOVE, LOSS, AND REDEMPTION

Edited by
DANIEL JONES

B \ D \ W \ Y
BROADWAY BOOKS
NEW YORK

Originally published in paperback by Three Rivers Press, an imprint of
Random House, a division of Penguin Random House LLC, New York, in
2007.

The essays in this work were originally published in the "Modern Love"
column of *The New York Times*.

Due to space limitations, permissions credits appear on page 287.

Inquiries concerning permission to reprint any article or portion
thereof should be directed to The New York Times Company, c/o Pars
International, 253 West 35th Street, 7th Floor, New York, NY 10001 or
NYTPermissions@Parsintl.com.

Library of Congress Cataloging-in-Publication Data is available upon
request.

ISBN 978-0-593-13704-8
Ebook ISBN 978-0-593-13705-5
Media Tie-In ISBN 978-0-593-13720-8

Printed in the United States of America

10 9 8 7

2019 Revised Edition

CONTENTS

HOLDING ON THROUGH THE CURVES

INTRODUCTION

What is a love story? As the editor of the "Modern Love" column, I ask myself that question all the time. When working my way through the eight-thousand-plus personal essay submissions that pour in every year, I am constantly forced to think: Is this a love story? Is that? If *The New York Times* is the newspaper of record, does that mean I'm choosing the love stories of record? If so, I'd better at least have a working definition.

When "Modern Love" began back in 2004, we founding editors of the column (Styles editor Trip Gabriel; my wife, Cathi Hanauer; and I) decided we would interpret "love" broadly because we didn't want to limit the stories to romantic love. We hoped the stories would explore the darkness as much as the light, plumb both the joys and the pain that spring from our lifelong efforts to be intimate with other human beings.

The most powerful stories typically involved relationships that had some mileage: the trials of midlife marriage, the strains of parenthood, and the loss of loved ones (children, spouses, parents, friends). These stories seldom celebrate roses and kisses, but are they love stories? Absolutely.

Vulnerability is the animating quality of all love stories, and it can take many forms. In every case, though, vulnerability means exposing ourselves to the possibility of loss, but also—crucially!—to the possibility of connection. You can't have one without the other. The stakes vary, of course, from dipping one's toe in the water to taking a blind dive from a high cliff.

Rachel Fields, in her essay "The Five Stages of Ghosting Grief," details her mounting anxiety after sending her first mildly sexual text message to a new guy she's started seeing and then waiting, in agony, for him to respond. For hours. Which might as well have been a lifetime. A different kind of vulnerability is on display in Amy Krouse Rosenthal's "You May Want to Marry My Husband," in which she writes a kind of dating profile for her husband because she's dying from ovarian cancer and doesn't want him to be alone after she's gone.

I suppose if we are going to try to define what a love story is, we should begin by defining what love is, but that can be even more slippery. Our definitions of love, too, tend toward the flowery treatment. From where I sit, however— as someone who has read, skimmed, or otherwise digested some one hundred thousand love stories over the past fifteen years—love, at its best, is more of a wheelbarrow than a rose: gritty and messy but also durable. Yet still hard to put into words.

Once, at the start of a radio interview, the host introduced me as the "Modern Love" editor and then asked, as her first question: "So what is love?"

I was so caught off guard, I laughed nervously and then said, "You're really going to open with that?" When she didn't laugh, we shared an awkward moment before I mumbled some generalities about human connection.

I wish I'd remembered how I had already answered that question in the "Modern Love" column a few years before, when I stepped into the space as editor during Valentine's week to note some observations. Because love, for me, is less about definitions than examples. Which is why I think the kaleidoscope of experiences represented in the "Modern Love" column, and in this book, can do the job better than any dictionary. Back then I wrote:

> If I were Spock from *Star Trek*, I would explain that human love is a combination of three emotions or impulses: desire, vulnerability, and bravery. Desire makes one feel vulnerable, which then requires one to be brave.
>
> Since I'm not Spock, I will tell a story.
>
> Say you decide to adopt a baby girl in China. You receive her photo, put it on your refrigerator, and gaze at it as the months pass, until finally you're halfway around the world, holding her in your arms, tears of joy streaming down your face.
>
> But later in your hotel room, after undressing her, you discover worrisome physical signs, in particular a scar on her spine. You call the doctor, then head to the hospital for examinations and CT scans,

where you are told the following: She suffered botched spinal surgery that caused nerve damage. Soon she will lose all bladder and bowel control. Oh, and she will be paralyzed for life. We're so sorry.

The adoption agency offers you a choice: keep this damaged baby or trade her in for a healthier one.

You don't even know about the trials yet to come, about the alarming diagnoses she'll receive back home, the terrifying seizures you'll witness. Nor do you know about the happy ending that is years off, when she comes through it all and is perfectly fine. You have to decide now. This is your test. What do you do?

If you're Elizabeth Fitzsimons, who told this story here one Mother's Day, you say: "We don't want another baby. We want our baby, the one sleeping right over there. She's our daughter."

That's love. Anyone can have it. All it requires is a little bravery. Or a lot.

If you're looking for random acts of bravery, including Elizabeth's, you'll find them in these pages. These tales shock and instruct. They provoke laughter and heartache and tears. Occasionally (it's true) they aren't even very modern. Always they pry open the oyster shell of human love to reveal the dark beauty within.

—Daniel Jones

SOMEWHERE
OUT THERE

SINGLE, UNEMPLOYED, AND SUDDENLY MYSELF

MARISA LASCHER

I WAS THIRTY-SEVEN, SINGLE, UNEMPLOYED, AND depressed because in a couple of months I was going to be moving out of my studio apartment on East 23rd Street in Manhattan and in with my mother in Sheepshead Bay, Brooklyn. Since taking a buyout at my Wall Street firm, I had devoted myself to two activities: searching for a new job and working out. And I spent a lot of time in my apartment.

So did the three recent college graduates next door. At their weekend parties, a loud bass penetrated our shared wall starting at 10:30 p.m. In sweats, no makeup, and with my hair piled in a bun, I would go out and ring their bell around 11 p.m. (early, even by my geriatric standards) to ask them to quiet down.

One of them would appear, flush with alcohol and annoyance, and promise to turn it down. Usually they did.

When they didn't, I would call the doorman, the management company, and, once, the police. But the noise continued.

My 23rd Street building was near three colleges. When I signed the lease, I didn't realize the place had so many student renters, people who understandably liked to party. Yet it was the least social time in my life. Most of my friends were married. I had no income, and rent was almost $3,000 a month. I wasn't dating because I hadn't figured out how to positively spin my unemployment story.

One afternoon in the elevator, I saw one of the guys from next door in jeans and a T-shirt, his dark hair slightly receding.

"Are you always around in the middle of the day?" he asked.

"For the last few months I have been," I said. "I'm job searching."

"I am too," he said. "It's my last year of law school."

"Never leave a job without another," I told him. People had warned me about this, but it was only after I'd done it that I realized how true it was. As we neared our doors, I said, "I'm moving out, so you guys can blast your music all night long. The mean old lady is leaving."

"Why?" he asked.

"I can't afford this any longer. I'm moving in with my mom in Brooklyn."

"That sucks," he said, then added: "It's not me blasting music. It's my roommates."

Which made sense. He was always the kindest and most apologetic when I got angry. "How old are you guys?" I said. "Like, twenty-three?"

"Yeah, well, I'm twenty-three," he said.

"I'm thirty-seven. So I hope you get a younger neighbor the next go-round."

"I never would have guessed thirty-seven," he said. "I thought you were, like, twenty-six."

Was he sweet-talking me? I looked the same age as my friends, but maybe the dormlike context had fooled him. That afternoon we ran into each other again; he was in a suit headed to an interview. I wished him luck.

Two weeks later, my friend Diana and I were sitting at a nearby bar, drinking vodka sodas, and looking at her Tinder app, when my twenty-three-year-old neighbor popped up.

"Swipe right!" I said. "Tell him you're out with me."

She swiped, they matched, and she told him I was with her. I followed up with a text, proud to be out on a Saturday night. Here was proof that I, too, was fun. We messaged back and forth; he was on his way home. When I asked if he wanted to join us back at my apartment, he said yes.

Twenty minutes later Diana and I arrived, and he showed up with a bottle of vodka and cans of Diet Coke.

Soon he was laughing, saying, "My roommates can't stand you. And I was always so confused why a twenty-six-year-old was upset about our parties. I thought you were just an old soul."

Diana and I danced to "Jump" by the Pointer Sisters, a song he didn't recognize. Before Diana left at 4 a.m., she whispered to me, "He likes you. Hook up."

I offered a hushed protest, insisting he was too young. But apparently the neighborly tension had been building, because he and I started kissing right after she left.

When we woke up, hung over, a few hours later, I begged him not to tell his roommates. My transformation from puritanical noise warden to Mrs. Robinson embarrassed me; my dulled brain screamed, "What just happened?"

But I won't lie: It was also an ego boost. I may not have had a job, a husband, or a boyfriend, but at least I could attract an adorable twenty-three-year-old.

Over the next few weeks, we texted constantly and kept getting together to talk about our dating and employment searches and to fool around. When I asked him if I seemed older, he said, "Not really. Mostly because you aren't working and you're around all of the time."

I said: "When I graduated high school, you were four."

One Sunday at 5 a.m., he got to experience the pleasure of being woken up in my bed by his roommates' drunken rendition of "Oops! . . . I Did It Again."

"This is really annoying," he yelled, covering his head with my pillow.

"It's payback," I said. "Now you understand."

With him, my usual romantic anxiety disappeared. Instead of projecting my insecurities onto him and wondering if I was enough, I just had fun because I knew our age gap made a future impossible. And I was moving out soon.

Not that my mind was entirely free of concerns. I worried people would think we were ridiculous. But when I told my coupled-up girlfriends, they said I was living a fantasy.

"At least you're having fun," a soon-to-be-divorced friend said. "None of us are. I didn't even want to touch my husband at the end."

Even so, the chasm between my new friend and me was no more glaring than when he said, "Dating is fun. I get to meet lots of people."

Dating, for me, was about as fun as my job search. And that was because I approached both in almost exactly the same way: with a strategy, spreadsheets, and a lot of anxiety about presenting my best self and hiding my weaknesses. With him, though, I worried about none of that.

When he admitted he had no idea what he was doing with women and made things up as he went along, I assured him this wouldn't change—no one knew.

Our honest exchange was so refreshing. Dates my age disguised their fears with arrogance. Within an hour of meeting me, one had boasted about the amount of sex he'd had, and another, on our second date, gave me a heads-up that his large size had caused many of his relationships to end. How considerate of him to warn me!

With appropriate romantic prospects, I had been overly polished and protective. Just like the men, I spun stories broadcasting fake confidence. But I confided in my neighbor about how hard the year had been and how worried I was about finding a job and a man to love. With nothing at stake, I was charmingly vulnerable.

One evening as we cuddled in my apartment, with me droning on about my man troubles and career fears, he said, "We get so fixated on the job we want or the person we're dating because we don't think there will be another. But there's always another."

I thought that was so true. Even wise. But it's easier to have that attitude, about jobs or love, at twenty-three than at thirty-seven.

Then one night I came home a little too drunk and encountered him in the hallway. He was the one who almost always decided when we would hang out, and I complained it wasn't fair that everything seemed to be on his terms. I was pressuring him, reverting to my worst dating default behavior, and he fled into his apartment.

The next day he texted: "maybe we should chill with this. you've been a good friend . . . we complicated it a little though haha."

I knew "haha" was just his millennial way of keeping it light, but here's the thing: In our "light" relationship, I had let myself be fully known, revealing all of my imperfections, in a way I normally didn't. With him I was my true self, and it was a revelation.

And a conundrum. Because I can't seem to be my true self when I'm seriously looking for love, when all I'm thinking about is the future. To win the person (or the job, for that matter), we think we have to be the most perfect version of ourselves. When our hearts are on the line, vulnerability can feel impossible.

A year later, I finally managed to be just perfect enough to land a job. I'm still working on allowing myself to be imperfect enough to find love.

Marisa Lascher lives in Manhattan and is a leader in designing empathy-based approaches to strengthen organizational culture and employee performance. This essay appeared in October 2017.

UH, HONEY, THAT'S NOT YOUR LINE

MATTESON PERRY

M OONLIGHT FROM THE WINDOW ILLUMINATED the tattoo of a phoenix covering the left side of her torso. I traced it with my finger, from just below her armpit, over the speed bumps of her ribs, to her hip bone. I had only seen tattoos like this in the movies, never in person, never this close, and never in my own bed.

I knew I had found my very own Manic Pixie Dream Girl.

When he was the film critic of the A.V. Club, Nathan Rabin coined the term "Manic Pixie Dream Girl" to describe the love interest in Cameron Crowe's *Elizabethtown*, though the character type has been in many movies before and since (Natalie Portman in *Garden State* being perhaps the quintessential example).

The Manic Pixie Dream Girl is now an indie-film cliché, more a collection of quirks than a person, who exists to be the perfect love interest for the male protagonist. These weird (but beautiful) girls appreciate shy, sad, creative boys and teach them to enjoy life again though sex, love, and various activities done in the rain.

Though often perky, the Manic Pixie Dream Girl will be troubled as well. She straddles the narrow line between quirky and crazy, mysterious and strange, sexy and slutty; she is perfectly imperfect. And that imperfection is the key, because a Manic Pixie Dream Girl must be messed up enough to need saving, so the powerless guy can do something heroic in the third act.

I met my Manic Pixie Dream Girl in a sketch comedy class. On the first day she wore a bright red dress and cowboy boots as if attired by the costume department. She had the olive skin and dark eyes of her half-Mexican lineage, a look one might describe as "exotic," though she would punch you in the arm if you used that term. She had a boyfriend, so we couldn't date, but we chatted online, learning about each other's lives while we traded YouTube clips of our favorite *Saturday Night Live* sketches.

One hot summer afternoon, we met at a bar with the intention of writing sketches together, but our plans changed, as they often do with Manic Pixie Dream Girls. We never opened our notebooks and instead went on an impromptu bar crawl.

Each new bar found us a bit drunker and sitting closer together. Our knees touched under tables and our shoulders brushed together as we walked. We sat so close I could smell her sweat, though the chemicals of infatuation turned it into a sweet perfume.

The night ended with a drunken attempted kiss by me, which she ducked under.

"I can't cheat on my boyfriend," she said. "Even if things aren't going well."

Not going well. I had hope. More than hope, it turned out. Within a month she broke up with him, and not long after she and her tattoo ended up in my bed.

I'm not a nerd by any means, but I've never been cool in the classic rebel way. For example, I secretly enjoy doing my taxes. This girl, though, was cool. She could get a drink at a hopelessly crowded bar. At parties she enchanted men with jokes and dancing and loud laughter. I could see the envy in their eyes when she left with me.

She made me feel cool by proxy, like a human VIP pass. Impulsive, erratic, and electric, she was my opposite, and the juxtaposition thrilled me. I fell deeply in love. And she loved me back.

My Manic Pixie Dream Girl was either all-in or all-out on everything she did, so things moved quickly. Within a year we moved to Los Angeles, where we lived together. I had never lived with a woman before and loved the intimacy it brought, but the domesticity troubled her. She began to freak out periodically about our future together.

Whatever the cause (the purchase of dining room chairs sparked the first), these freak-outs followed the same script. She would cry and yell and pace around the apartment while declaring us incompatible. I would stay calm and explain how our differences made us work so well together by strengthening each other's weaknesses.

I always justified why she shouldn't be freaking out,

why we should be together, in essence, why her feelings were "wrong." (Shocker: People's feelings are never wrong.) I didn't mind the episodes so much. I considered them the symptom of my Manic Pixie Dream Girl being perfectly imperfect.

As we approached three years together, she struggled with a bout of depression, and it created a rift between us. We had been a couple that did everything together, but she started going out without me.

On several occasions I woke up at three or four in the morning to find she wasn't home yet and hadn't called. I would lie in bed, vacillating between worry and anger, calling her every half hour. If she answered, she would usually refuse my offer to pick her up and say something like, "No, I'm still having fun here."

Sometimes I didn't know where "here" was, if "here" belonged to a guy or a girl.

In the morning I would question her whereabouts, more disapproving parent than angry lover, playing my role of the calm, rational, square boyfriend. She would just nod, say a perfunctory sorry, and go to sleep. At night she was the Manic Pixie Dream Girl for other people; during the day I got the Hungover Depressed Pixie Nightmare. I knew our relationship was in trouble, but I still loved her and believed this was just the difficult third act before "happily ever after."

One weekend I went camping with friends, trying to give her space. Before I left I wrote her a letter (five pages, single-spaced) about our relationship. I told her how much I loved her, how I wouldn't stop fighting for "us," and concluded by saying, "I know my love can't fix your depression, but I still want you to know my love's here and always will be."

I put the letter on her desk with flowers and departed. I spent the twelve-hour drive to Lake Powell waiting for her to call, but the phone just sat in the cup holder, silent for hours and hours. Late in the afternoon it finally beeped—not a call, but a text message. She thanked me for the flowers and didn't even mention the letter. I knew then our relationship was over.

While the Manic Pixie Dream Girl always rescues the man from the doldrums of life in the first act of the movie, the roles reverse in the end, with him ultimately saving her with his love. Beyond the coolness and excitement they bestow, this is the true gift of the Manic Pixie Dream Girl, because fixing something, especially when it's a person, is what makes a man feel most valuable.

When I said in my letter I knew my love couldn't fix her depression, I was lying. I thought my love could fix everything, including her depression. That letter was my Grand Gesture, the one that saves the relationship and the girl. It was my Lloyd Dobler moment, holding a boom box over my head, blasting "In Your Eyes."

In the movies the romantic gesture works, but it failed me in real life. This was like Diane Court coming to the window only to shut it so she could go back to sleep. I gave her my heart; she thanked me for the $12.99 flowers.

What makes movies magical is not that incredible things happen in them. Incredible things happen in real life. No, what makes movies magical is they end right after the incredible thing happens. They stop after the war is over, after the team wins the game, after the boy gets the girl. But in life the story keeps going and the boy can later lose the girl. "Happily ever after" is too boring for a Manic Pixie Dream Girl.

Not long after I returned from my trip, she dumped me. There would be no effort to save the relationship; no longer all-in, she was all-out. It seemed my love couldn't "fix" her after all, and even worse, she didn't want to be fixed. Needing to be repaired is the No. 1 rule of being a Manic Pixie Dream Girl—how could she ignore it?

She could ignore it because she wasn't a Manic Pixie Dream Girl. She wasn't a character or plot device in my story, or some damaged creature with deep despair that I and only I could cure as part of my "hero's journey." She was simply someone who had fallen out of love with her boyfriend. Which happens. It's really uncinematic, but it happens.

So our story ended, not with credits rolling to freeze our relationship in eternal bliss, but with crying and the division of possessions. (I kept the dining room chairs; she kept the old-timey typewriters.) It took a while, but I found someone new.

This time I'm trying to make ours an original love story instead of one I stole from the movies.

Matteson Perry is a writer and performer in Los Angeles, where he lives with his wife, the "someone new" from the end of this essay, which appeared in July 2013.

I SEEMED PLUCKY AND GAME, EVEN TO MYSELF

MINDY HUNG

I AM A GOOD, PRACTICAL GIRL. I EAT MY VEGETA-bles. I go to bed early. In fact, at thirty-one, I'm not just good, I'm an apprehensive priss—and I hate it.

In a recent attempt to invent a brave new me, I contacted Tom on an online dating website. Something had to change. *I* had to change. On free evenings, I tend to gravitate toward bookstores rather than bar stools. I walk with my head plunged forward and my eyes down. I'm hardly a hermit; I have plenty of friends, take solo trips to Europe (with my agenda fussily planned out, of course), and fill my weekends with brunches and shows. But my romantic life has been tepid at best, usually stalled out by my caution and timidity.

Friends urged me to try Internet dating, and at first I was wary, but soon I realized I'd found the perfect medium. I could be an extrovert without the exertion. And suddenly I was popular: I seemed to appeal to males from Hawaii to

Virginia. Musicians, marathoners, soldiers, brokers, a man who claimed to own five "Rolix" watches, a Hollywood dentist—all these men and more wrote to me and professed their interest. Their attention gave me a shot of bravery—or bravado, at least. They didn't know about my anxious, twittering self. They thought I was exciting. Maybe I was.

Tom's profile began unremarkably: he loved Australia, clean sheets, and orange juice. But midway through, he charmed me by confessing that he'd deleted an entire paragraph because he feared he was sounding like the kind of rambling and often incoherent messages that he sometimes left on people's answering machines.

I looked at this wry, sheepish admission, and I understood completely. What's more, I knew exactly how to respond.

"You seem very good at the charming, self-deprecating schtick," I teased in my introductory e-mail. "Do you blush and stutter in person?" I gave him my number, unasked.

A few days later he called, and as we bantered on the phone I surprised myself by asking him out. I chose the time (Saturday at 3:00 p.m.) and the place (Cha-An Teahouse, on East Ninth Street). I forwarded him instructions on which train to take, which direction to walk in when he left the station, and where to meet me in case it rained. I tried to sound nonchalant and in control, like I asked men out all the time.

Heading out for our date, I wore a silk skirt and a low-cut shirt, and I brought a backpack. I was bound for Connecticut later that night with plans to go kayaking on Sunday. I seemed plucky and game, even to myself.

As I approached Cha-An, I saw Tom waiting out front—I

recognized those long eyelashes and easy smile from his picture. But in person he was disconcertingly self-assured. He didn't stutter or blush as I'd imagined. And he was apparently bold in other ways, too: he told me he'd once quit his job to become a professional gambler. When I told him about my kayaking plans, he instructed me on how to turn my clothing into a flotation device in case my kayak overturned.

All the while, for three hours, I remained confident, engaged, decidedly unprissy. My only slip came when he stopped and said, "You have two very deep dimples." There was a pause. "And now you're blushing."

I recovered and held up for the rest of the date, but the damage had been done, and my poise—or my pose—didn't last long. But, worse, instead of maintaining my cool, venturesome, see-what-happens demeanor, I promptly plunged into fantasizing about our future together: Tom and me playing Frisbee in the park, sharing a cupcake with chocolate frosting, running along the Hudson. I would slap his behind and take off giggling.

By the second date, I'd decided to abandon the carefree adventurer. I was going to be a great big flirt. I would bat my eyelashes, stroke his wrist, and work some coquettish magic.

We had agreed to go out for Indian food in Curry Hill. I brought him two Aero bars because he'd told me that he liked English chocolates. His eyes lit up when I pulled out the candy. "You might be the perfect woman for me," he said. Or maybe not. Because then he talked about Nicole Kidman and other blondes he had crushes on. I concentrated on cooing and nodding my decidedly unblond head.

I was too focused on trying to secure my vision to realize that I was acting like a fool. If I'd been using my head, I would have noticed the warning signs: all the talk about ex-girlfriends and his complaints about the terrible women on the dating website . . . Tom was not interested—or not interested enough.

After dinner, I invited him to my apartment, where I made tea. He stretched out on the sofa and put his feet on the coffee table. I scooted up close to him. He pulled away.

He was nervous, he said. Women were unpredictable. He wanted to be honest. "I find you attractive," he said, "but I don't see this being long-term." Then he gave me a sideways glance and added, "I wouldn't be opposed to a fling."

I felt numb. Bold me might have asked what the hell gave him the right to make up his mind so quickly. But I wasn't a spunky fighter after all, was I?

Instead, I slumped on the couch. I wanted more; I'd acted like an agreeable, love-struck half-wit all evening in order to get it. I had no poses left.

Tom seemed a little sad, but nonetheless he guided me into the bedroom, where he laid me down and put his arms around me. "I feel like a jerk," he said, touching the skin of my stomach. "We could always just be friends. We don't need to have a fling at all."

I blinked twice and propped myself up on one elbow. "Oh no, I'd like to have the sex," I said crisply, "but I don't see how we could ever be friends. The sex thing would always get in the way."

There was a pause. Apparently, this was rather original of me. This was also rather insane of me. Tom laughed. For the first time that evening, he eyed me with what seemed like admiration. "That's usually my line," he said.

I'd gotten my game back. In one audacious move, I had regained my self-respect and control of my brain—or so I thought. We batted the idea around some more and decided that I should think it over. I walked Tom to the subway station. As we parted, I told him I would call him. He said that would be best and kissed me on the forehead.

The next morning, I got up and ran four miles. Then I went back to bed and curled up in a fetal position.

I could still be an adventurous me, I reasoned from the safety of my covers. I thought about Tom's eyes peering at me from under his long lashes. The more I brooded about it, the more a fling seemed like a good idea: I had a healthy libido, a year's supply of birth control pills, and several changes of sheets. If I could detach myself from the disappointment over the lack of long-term interest in me, I might have fun. Never mind that I'd spent the day in bed moping over a boy like a decidedly undetached and unfun girl.

I fired off an e-mail:

OK, so I've thought this through. Fling is fine. Iffy about the friends thing, though. I'm not sure that I like you very much right now. Plus, although I am familiar with the general concept, I am not sure how this particular specific friendship would play out in real life. What would we do? Play catch in the park? Get manicures together? Anyway, Barbara Ehrenreich is reading at Barnes and Noble Union Square on Wednesday at 7. Interested in going?

I read my note. It seemed casual. It conveyed some anger, yes, yet I seemed detached, frank, witty, intelligent.

I was, of course, just confusing.

"I'm confused by your message," Tom wrote. "If you don't like me very much, why do you want to keep seeing me? I don't very much like not being liked very much!"

Okay, perhaps I hadn't come across as the adventurous, ready-for-trouble woman I'd intended. Perhaps I'd come across as a bitter, scary nutcase.

I can fix this, I thought, rubbing my hands together. But I wasn't sure what I wanted to repair: The potential fling? Or the potential friendship?

I started typing. I explained that although I was drawn to him, I couldn't possibly like him. I had to remain cold in order to avoid being hurt. Surely, he would understand. "I'd like to see how this experiment turns out," I wrote in conclusion. "The question is, do you?"

I reread the e-mail: it was honest, vulnerable, and realistic, with no obvious spelling mistakes. I hit Send.

This time, it only took me two hours to understand that I'd written another crazy message. I wasn't a bold explorer in the sea of love. I was the same timid girl I'd always been, just working a little harder this time to avoid heartbreak.

Tom never replied.

My friend Dwight tells me that craziness is what ensues when two clear and opposing visions collide. He is referring to Tom's fling plans versus my dewy vignettes of the future. Dwight is married. He can be objective. He says that my wild responses were a natural reaction to an unfair proposition.

I don't know. Perhaps my expectations—for a relationship, and for myself—were as unreasonable as Tom's. Based on one date and a phone call, I had envisioned a future of endless summers: green lawns, cupcakes, and Tom running beside a blithe, smiling me. The only thing less real than Tom's presence in my idyll was the brassy yet carefree version of myself I saw bounding along beside him.

Mindy Hung lives in New York City, where she writes romance novels as Ruby Lang. Her latest release is Playing House. *This essay appeared in November 2005.*

AT THE HOSPITAL, AN INTERLUDE OF CLARITY

BRIAN GITTIS

THERE IS NEVER A GOOD TIME TO FALL OFF YOUR couch onto a martini glass, nick a major blood vessel, and begin losing a dangerous amount of blood, but having this happen in the middle of a promising date is an especially bad time. Nothing breaks the mysterious spell of blossoming attraction faster than spurting blood.

I demonstrated this last spring while on my fourth date with a Brazilian woman so beautiful I was almost afraid of her. After dinner in a homey Italian restaurant, we walked back to the apartment I had just moved into in Brooklyn. Living in the city for the first time without roommates, I was eager to take advantage of my newfound privacy. And things were going well. There's something romantic about drinking from fancy glasses in an unfurnished room full of unpacked boxes. Miles Davis's *In a Silent Way* spun on the record player.

I was amazed to have gotten this far. As my friends were sick of hearing, it made no sense to me that a gorgeous woman in her early twenties who spoke four languages and had lived on three continents was spending her Saturdays with me, a thirty-one-year-old bookish type from Pittsburgh.

Each outing felt as if I were sneaking into an exclusive club, and at the end of the night I always feared I would be discovered and asked to leave. I realize that meeting someone wonderful is the whole point of dating, but actually being with someone wonderful can be too stressful for me to enjoy.

This stress is typical for me. I have been on anti-anxiety medication for about ten years, and on dates I'm constantly asking myself: "Was that the wrong thing to say? Do I seem nervous? Will obsessing about being nervous make me appear more nervous?"

Not unusual questions to ask yourself when meeting new people, but for me they can be paralyzing. Any brain space left for experiencing the date itself is woefully small. Even if the evening goes well, I often appreciate it only later and from a distance, as if it had happened to someone else— like dating in the third person.

So far my success with this particular woman had been an exercise in ignoring the reality of it, which apparently also led me to ignore the reality of my surroundings in general. As she unraveled herself from our embrace on the couch to use the bathroom, I fell onto the after-dinner drink she had left on the floor, the glass slicing into the soft underside of my upper arm. When I looked down, I glimpsed my exposed triceps and more blood than I had ever seen in my life. The cut had gone nearly to the bone.

This is not the first time a date ended with me in the emergency room. I seem to have a knack for it. My college girlfriend once served undercooked chicken that gave me hallucinations and a fever of 104. Years later, my attempt to cook breakfast for another woman ended in second-degree burns after I managed to set fire to a paper towel. But the severity of this injury, its unfortunate timing, and the fact that I was naked all broke new ground.

In the ambulance, the emergency medical workers held together my arm, but their questions threatened to unravel my subterfuge as an acceptable mate to this accomplished young woman.

"How old are you?" one asked, which put our substantial age difference—something we had not yet talked about— suddenly under a spotlight.

"Are you on any medication?"

"Antidepressants and Klonopin," I reluctantly answered.

Then, to her: "Is he your boyfriend? Your friend?"

Long pause. "Boyfriend," she blurted uncomfortably. Then, an instant later, "Friend."

Even though I was riding in an ambulance to surgery, that one still stung.

To the entertainment of the hospital's overnight staff, I was still half-naked when I arrived. My date had managed to get pants on me while we waited for the ambulance, but as I hadn't been able to let go of my arm at the time, my shirt would go on only halfway. Being wheeled into surgery like this, alongside a woman in a sexy dress, pretty much screamed "sex injury."

The next hour was a chaotic blur of X-rays, questions I

struggled not to panic about (why does this waiver form ask for my religious preference?), and several doctors' disconcertingly wide-eyed reactions to my injury.

When I asked, "I'm not going to lose my arm, am I?" the answer was a troubling, "I don't think so."

A brusque surgeon with a pitiless stare prodded me as he mumbled about my case to a flock of residents. I couldn't hear everything, but "seven centimeters" and "arterial" came through loud and clear.

Physical humiliation was next on the agenda. Before the operation, my date got to watch a nurse move my pasty, fluorescent-lit body out of my bloody jeans and into a hospital gown. I pictured us sitting at dinner a week from now, this unflattering snapshot of me hovering between us as I pointed at what I wanted on the menu to the waiter with my hook arm.

Then it was time. I remember that the lights in the operating room were very bright, and I remember being told they were about to start the anesthesia. And suddenly: oblivion.

I awoke in a haze. My arm, and my date, were both still with me. The operation had gone well, but protocol required me to stay in the emergency room for six more hours. This registered, briefly, as a terrifying amount of time for a woman and me to be left alone with no dim lighting, no alcohol, no movie to watch or appetizers to eat, and no escape hatch in the event of awkwardness.

Anxiety visits some people in violent bursts, like an electrical storm. For me, it creeps in gradually and insidiously, like a thickening fog. When the fog becomes dense enough, it causes a scary, dreamlike sensation that my psychiatrist calls "derealization," where I kind of shut down and can no longer really function in a social situation.

That moment in the hospital should have been one when the fog began its creep, but for some reason it stayed away. I'll never know if my calm was psychological (a cocktail of adrenaline, morphine, and utter relief) or physiological; after six hours of unbroken embarrassment and fear, I was simply too exhausted.

Whatever the reason, I felt fine. My thoughts were clear and unencumbered. My date's eyes stared into mine with an uncomplicated tenderness that made my head swim. It was as if we had jumped forward years, and the anxieties and gamesmanship of our early dates were a quaint and distant memory. *This*, I thought, *is what it's like to be with this woman.* Neither of us had changed, but I was in a different world.

Those six hours sailed by gloriously. We traded hospital stories and endless jokes about martini glasses. We talked about books and our families. We came up with an absurd screenplay idea, a horror movie set in a hospital. I was talking and laughing and effortlessly connecting with one of the most beautiful women I had ever seen, a woman I was truly falling for.

When I was finally released, our midmorning cab ride back to my neighborhood felt like a lucid dream. We ate egg sandwiches in the park and returned to find the familiar surroundings of my living room splattered with blood. Through a haze of sleep deprivation and residual morphine, I felt like a ghost returning to the scene of my own murder.

As we stood there, mopping up bloody footprints with our Swiffers, surrounded by wadded-up pink paper towels,

I thought, *Either you will never see this woman again, or she will stick around a long time.*

Neither happened. I would like to be able to say my story ends in an epiphany, with the end of my anxiety and the beginning of an enduring relationship. But the reality is she left me about a month later. Not because she had found me repulsive in the fluorescent light of the hospital, but for a more conventional reason: She missed her ex-boyfriend.

Sometimes when a guy really likes a girl, he gets a tattoo on his arm. I got this prominent scar instead. But there are times when I finger its deep groove (a new nervous tic), those six beautiful hours in the emergency room flicker in my head, and I am reminded how close I am to an alternate world in which I am happy, a world that occupies the same space as this one but is somehow distinct from it. And while that better world may be difficult to find, it is as close to me as the air in front of my face.

Brian Gittis works in book publishing and lives in New Jersey with his wife and son. This essay appeared in October 2014.

THE FIVE STAGES OF GHOSTING GRIEF

RACHEL FIELDS

AT 6:30 A.M. I WAS BLOW-DRYING MY HAIR, GET-ting ready for work, and accepting the demise of my two-week relationship. The nail in the coffin was that at ten the night before I had texted him something vaguely sexual, and he hadn't texted back.

The morning had become a quick but emotionally turbulent journey through the five stages of grief.

First: denial. It was entirely possible he hadn't seen the text. He could have been in a deep sleep. He could have dropped his phone in the toilet. He could have died! Any of these options were comforting.

He wasn't really a texter anyway, so his lack of response didn't necessarily reflect the weirdness of my text. It was probably normal for non-texters to see a text and not reply to it. They saw it, found it charming (or not), but didn't think it required a response. Totally standard.

Anyway, was the text even that weird? If you went on a date and got vaguely physical during a make-out session on a bench in a secluded area of a public park, wouldn't it seem natural to text something vaguely sexual a few days afterward?

I opened my messages to remind myself what exactly I had sent. There it was, at 10:02 p.m.: "I can't stop thinking about what I'm now referring to as 'bench time.'"

OK, so it was a little confusing. Deep into my third glass of wine, I had thought I was being coy, but the result was somewhat inscrutable. It wasn't even clear I had enjoyed the experience. Was it possible he thought I was traumatized? Did he think I was accusing him of something?

No, that was ridiculous. He probably had noted my text, smiled, felt as aroused as you can be by a text as vaguely sexual as mine was, and gone to sleep, dreaming of me.

But all the same, isn't it a little rude to get a text from a woman you've been dating for two weeks and not even acknowledge it? How hard can it be to fire off a blushing smiley emoji or a four-word answer? He didn't even need to reciprocate the sexual innuendo (though it would have been appreciated). He could have just said, "Nice."

(Scrap that. "Nice" would have been way worse. If he had texted "Nice," I would have thrown myself into the sea.)

I didn't care if he was a non-texter—and what does that even mean in this day and age? If you're a twenty-something urban professional who doesn't text, you're pretty much impossible to be friends with. For a friendship to exist in 2015, people need to know they can text "ugh I love oysterrrrs" at 2:15 p.m. on a Friday and get a response by 2:30.

Of course, there would be pathetically little at stake if he failed to reply to a Friday afternoon "ugh I love oysterrrrs" text. But this was my first flirtatious text after our first physical encounter. By not responding, he was essentially shouting into the universe, "You are overly sexual, way too forward, and deeply unattractive to me."

But honestly, if he was offended, I didn't want to be dating him anyway. You can't engage in an open-shirted make-out session and then get offended when the woman texts you a vaguely (vaguely!) sexual follow-up.

Maybe if I didn't look at my phone for the next five minutes, he would text. Yes, that was the answer. I would blow-dry my hair like a casual, confident, independent woman. I would think about work and my friends and whether I should make an appointment for . . . Seriously, had he still not texted?

I put my phone facedown with the ringer off. Now I couldn't see if he texted, and I could start living my life. I was single, empowered, and ready for anything.

No, that wouldn't work. If the ringer was off and the phone was facedown, I wouldn't know if he did text. The best solution was to keep the phone faceup, ringer off, so I could see the phone light up if he texted—but not be bothered by the ringer. The ring tone was jarring, and anyway I was blow-drying my hair, so I wouldn't hear it.

Two minutes later, still no text.

I started thinking about my life and what it might look like from the outside. Two nights before, he and I had stood gazing at the Chicago Botanic Garden's much-discussed corpse flower, which had been due to bloom that evening but hadn't.

"This plant looks fake," he had said. "It looks like a plant from a 1930s movie about prehistoric jungles. How do we know this thing is real?"

I laughed. "Maybe it's just a ruse to get visitors, and the plant is made of plastic. No one would know."

The room was still. Dusk was nearly upon us and a strong rainstorm had kept away the evening crowds. Happiness stole over me, the quiet joy of standing in the dark in front of a six-foot-tall plant, talking in unnecessary whispers.

"What if it blooms right now?" I said. "What if it blooms and we're the only ones to witness it?" The thought made me shiver. As rain pounded the walls outside, I wanted nothing more than for the corpse flower to bloom for us alone.

A security guard at the door interrupted my fantasy. He peered into the room and glared at us.

"Closing time," he barked. "You would've been locked in here all night."

"Sorry, sir," I said, and we followed him out, suppressing our laughter.

Yes, I thought it had gone well. When we parted on the train platform, I had felt sure we would go out again. It was early to feel so confident, yes, but in the happy haze of our four hours together, I had pictured us months down the road, walking hand in hand along a Chicago street. I had imagined him really liking me.

But as I surveyed my apartment—towel still on the bed, Walmart lamp from college in the corner—I started to reconsider. I am messy, lazy, and selectively kind. Other women have white sheets that are actually clean and little

bowls filled with decorative stones. Other women keep or-
chids. Other women do yoga.

I told myself this wasn't true and we all have flaws, but
I doubted other women's flaws were as bad as mine.

In the past, when I asked my friends about their faults,
they said things that didn't count: They got frustrated
sometimes or worked too much. These conversations inevitably ended with me saying, "Those aren't bad enough," and
storming away.

They didn't say what I wanted to hear. That deep down,
they weren't sure if they were likable. That they were so ir-
responsible, they couldn't imagine being mothers. They
didn't say they craved attention but had trouble giving it to
others. They didn't say how cruel they could be.

These were surely the flaws he had seen in me.

Switching the blow-dryer to the other side of my head, I
took a few deep breaths. What if he had seen my flaws and
hadn't texted because of them? What if he had seen who I
was and hadn't liked me? I tried to get beyond my immedi-
ate response (*If he doesn't like me, nobody likes me, and I am
unlikable*) and really think about it.

If he hadn't texted because he didn't like me, was that so
bad? Relationships shouldn't be about suckering people in
with some sanitized version of yourself, only to spring the
real you on them later.

Maybe he had seen the real me and decided I wasn't for
him. Plenty of things aren't for me: running, action movies,
owning a dog. None of those things are bad because I don't
like them.

And if he hadn't liked me, why would I want to be with
him? I wanted a relationship with someone who thought I

was wonderful. Messy, maybe. Prone to leaving towels on the bed, yes. Bad with money, absolutely. But wonderful.

Maybe he had seeds of doubt and realized what it takes a lot of other people years to figure out: that those seeds of doubt can spread tendrils through your body until they eventually strangle your heart. And then five years later, you're having dinner together and all you can think is, "This isn't right." But by then, it's too late.

It was better to take notice now and bow out gracefully. Better to save us both years of indecision, resentment, and desperation.

Maybe by not texting, he had given me the gift of the rest of my life.

I put down my blow-dryer and checked the time: 7:15. Outside, the breeze was lifting the leaves on the trees and traffic was starting to pick up.

There was only so much life to live, and no time to spend it with people who weren't the very best fit.

And then he texted.

Rachel Fields is a writer and marketer in Madison, Wisconsin. This essay appeared in November 2015.

MISERY LOVES FRIED CHICKEN, TOO

MARK McDEVITT

NATE WAS MY BREAKUP BUDDY. WE WERE INTRO-
duced at Scruffy Murphy's Irish Pub by a mutual friend
who thought we'd like each other. And I liked Nate instantly. With his tight crew cut and animated features, he
seemed transplanted from another generation. You could
easily imagine him as a bit player in a fifties war movie, yell-
ing out lines like "Hey, Sarge! Over here. He's inna hole!" or
"They shot me, Ma! I'm bleedin'!"

We hung out that summer evening in support of a favorite local band. But when our mutual friend left Florida for
Boston, and Nate started seeing a woman, our fledgling
friendship stalled out.

I was in a relationship then, too. She and I had been together for more than two years and had even begun to talk
about marriage, which both excited and terrified us. We
were approaching our thirties, so it seemed like the logical

next step. And then it all unraveled rather suddenly, leaving me angry and bewildered.

It was during this aftermath that I bumped into Nate again. At first I didn't quite recognize him. In the year since I'd seen him, he'd packed on a good twenty pounds and grown a scruffy beard. Gone were the once-animated features and zippy one-liners. Something about his hollowed-out stare and shellshocked appearance told me his relationship hadn't worked out, either. No surprise, then, that the place we ran into each other was the Self-help section of Barnes & Noble.

This time our bonding was instantaneous and absolute, the kind shared between shipwreck survivors on a bobbing yellow life raft. While no model of mental health myself, I at least had a couple of months' head start on Nate. For him, only weeks after his breakup, the world was still a minefield of painful associative memories: a sudden whiff of jasmine or an innocent radio jingle was apt to produce in him bouts of demented laughter or uncontrollable crying.

Over the next couple of months our friendship flourished. Favorite recipes for chili were exchanged, along with Patsy Cline records. We swapped our many self-help books, which we referred to with titles like *Men Are from Mars, Women Are for the Birds* and *Cohabitating No More*. I gave Nate the entire collector's edition of the Three Stooges; he gave me a cactus.

"These prickly little bastards is some tough hombres," he explained. "Just like you and me. We may be in the desert right now, but I'm here to tell ya that we'll get through this."

Over time our anger and despair gave way to confusion. Just what had happened anyway? Where did we go wrong?

Like a crack team of FAA investigators we scoured the crash sites of our respective disasters looking for clues. Details and timelines were relentlessly hashed over. But the cause of Nate's midair explosion remained as mysterious to us as the forces that had caused my own relationship to belly flop into the Everglades like a jumbo jet with the wings sheared off.

Our futile search for answers only deepened our depression, but the great thing about depression is that it's not one size fits all, but rather comes tailor-made to suit one's particular personality. For me it's about insomnia, skewed priorities, and loss of interest.

Food, work, correspondence, even the Three Stooges: all lose their luster. The big picture fades as minor details assume gargantuan proportions. CDs will suddenly beckon to be rearranged, from alphabetical to reverse chronological order and back again. I simply have no choice.

The only real consolation is found in pop music. Leonard Cohen, Elvis Costello, the Smiths: a never-ending cycle of misery and heartache providing grist for our mill of self-pity. Pop music has the amazing ability to make you feel depressed and hopeful at the same time: depressed that you identify with the sentiment, and hopeful because someone feels more miserable than you.

For me that someone was Nate. The only brightness to my day was seeing my breakup buddy and feeling marginally better that he was even more depressed than I. He'd show up at my door carrying a family-size bucket of chicken drumsticks. If I'd lost all interest in food, Nate had gone in the opposite direction; he gobbled up anything that wasn't fastened to the floor. Even so, he couldn't figure out his weight gain.

"I just don't get it," he'd say, wolfing down his third cheeseburger. "I mean, where did it all come from? It's like you turn thirty and *boom!* You're a pumpkin."

I suggested a little exercise. There were tennis courts near his apartment, and so it became our habit to play once or twice a week. Neither of us played well, but with a lot of sweating and grunting, it proved therapeutic.

When I aggravated an old shoulder injury, our tennis came to an end. After that I didn't hear from Nate for a couple of weeks, and I assumed he'd found another tennis partner or become busy at work. But when my phone calls and e-mail messages went unanswered, I decided to drive over to his apartment and check up on him. His car was there, but the blinds of his place were drawn. After I pounded on the door for a good fifteen minutes, Nate finally poked his head outside, like a giant mastodon awakened from a thousand-year slumber. Something about his glassy-eyed stare and the greenish-orange hue of his skin told me he'd taken a turn for the worse.

Walking into his darkened lair, I understood that Nate had not found another tennis partner. Instead he had crossed over into Joseph Conrad territory; he'd journeyed up the Nang River into the "Heart of Darkness."

Without air-conditioning, the apartment was a good ten degrees hotter than the ninety degrees it was outside. The fetid hum of sweat, unwashed clothing, and rotting food hung heavy in the air. A chicken carcass lay on the kitchen floor, stripped to the bone as if by piranha.

Walking to open a window, I noticed there were vegetable peelings all over the floor. Nate appeared moments later from the kitchen, mechanically shaving a carrot. When he finished, he chomped on the carrot and started peeling another.

"What's with the carrots?" I asked.

"Oh, nothing," he said. "I just quit smoking."

"And you took up carrots?"

"Gives me something to do with my hands."

I filled three garbage bags with chicken bones and pizza boxes and took them out to the Dumpster.

Smack in the middle of the living room, directly in front of the television, was a shiny new bench press and giant barbell. Glossy brochures and bright plastic folders about how to become a real estate millionaire in ten easy steps littered the floor. Gradually a picture began to emerge of a man who hadn't slept or washed in days, spending his time alternately lifting weights, watching late-night infomercials, and eating fried chicken.

Alarmed and anxious to get out of there, I suggested we go see a movie. He was game, and after stopping for two bags of carrots, we pulled into the theater.

The event movie of the summer was *Cast Away,* starring Tom Hanks as Chuck Noland, a clever chap who washes ashore on a desert island after his plane goes down in the Pacific. As his hope of rescue fades, he begins the long battle for survival and, more important, his sanity. Something about the story spoke directly to Nate and me.

While I don't think *Cast Away* was intended as a comedy, we never laughed so hard in all our lives. It was like

watching ourselves up there on-screen. People in the audience glared disapprovingly as we laughed in all the wrong
places. We howled when Chuck knocked out his tooth with
an ice skate. While the rest of the audience sniffled as he
selected the tree from which to hang himself, we clenched
our sides with hilarity.

Hopelessly isolated and lonely, Chuck develops a relationship with a volleyball, giving the ball a face, even a
name: Wilson. It is Wilson, more than anything, that helps
preserve his sanity, allowing him to mount a last desperate
bid to escape his island prison.

I thought about the strange set of circumstances and
coincidence that had brought Nate and me together. I told
myself he was fortunate to have me as a friend. And while
keeping an eye on him had allowed me to feel charitable
and magnanimous, I knew my impulse had been anything
but altruistic.

In truth, Nate was the yardstick by which I measured
my own progress, helping me to feel good about myself and
preserve my own sanity. Nate, I realized, had become my
Wilson. This overweight, slightly addled person munching
carrots next to me was my life raft.

When the movie ended, we shuffled outside with the
rest of the Saturday night date crowd: handsome boys and
coltish girls dressed in shorts and T-shirts. They wandered
outside, laughing and smiling, blissfully unaware of the
dangers they courted.

Would they still be happy and smiling in a year's time,
knowing as we did that to love is to risk great unhappiness?
For them the movie was over, forgotten like the too-large

buckets of popcorn left under their seats. For us the movie clung like a lingering dream state. It followed us into the parking lot and beyond.

After getting ice cream, Nate and I sat outside admiring the clear night sky, each happy to have company but secretly wishing that he was somewhere else, with someone else. I couldn't even recognize it for the glorious time it was.

Six months later I finally managed to escape my own desert island by moving to New York. And though I've since lost touch with Nate, I often think about him. When I do, it's not the grief of my horrible breakup I remember but the laughter and friendship that followed.

Don't believe me? Just ask Chuck Noland. I'm sure he feels the same way about Wilson.

Mark McDevitt is a writer and screenwriter. He lives with his family in New Jersey. This essay appeared in June 2005.

SO HE LOOKED LIKE DAD. IT WAS JUST DINNER, RIGHT?

ABBY SHER

THERE WAS THIS PROFESSOR NAMED ANDREW who studied artificial intelligence. He was very handsome, in a professorial way. He wore gray turtleneck sweaters and smelled like mint aftershave and old books. He was fifty-five and recently divorced for the second time. He was my father.

He wasn't really my father. My father died when I was eleven. But Andrew was handsome like my father. He whistled like my father. He had sideburns with little touches of silver, like my father. And he was the only other person besides my father who ever called me by my full name, Abigail. It means father's joy. People usually just call me Abby.

The first time I saw Andrew was at a staff meeting. I don't know exactly why I was at the meeting. I was working for the university's research lab as a "content specialist."

My job was mostly copying papers about studies on brain activity. On busy days I collated and stapled.

During the meeting I watched Andrew lean back in his chair. His eyes were dark gray, like his sweater. He was biting his lower lip and listening intently. He looked like a little boy and a grown man at the same time. He glanced up and caught me staring at him. He smiled.

The next day I saw him by the copy machine. He was walking back into his office. His door was open, and there was classical music playing softly, because he was a professor. The light that spilled from his doorway was warm, and I could hear him humming along with a violin. I wanted a reason to go inside, to see his desk, his books. Maybe he had a potted plant? Framed pictures of his past?

Later that week I saw him at the coffee shop in the basement of our office building. He had a large coffee and large hands. I said hello.

He said, "Abigail, right?"

"Yes."

We just stared at each other. He looked like he might leave, so I said, "Oh wow! You like coffee? I like coffee, too."

He laughed. He had a soft laugh. His teeth were strong-looking.

Pretty soon I was going to that copier by Andrew's office all the time. Often I had nothing to copy, so I would make copies of my driver's license, and then make copies of the copy. By the fifth copy my face was just two eyes peeking out of a blizzard.

One day, while I was standing by his door, copying my hand, Andrew came out and stood next to me.

"Do you like duck?" he asked.

"Hmmm, duck," I said. "Who doesn't like duck?"

"So would you like to have dinner sometime?"

We made plans for the next Tuesday.

Tuesday afternoon I went into his office when he was out and wrote my address on a scrap of paper. I left it by his daily planner. Notes are cute when you still have braces and are just discovering lip gloss and boys. Notes are different when you're leaving them on a mahogany desk with an ashtray and a glass paperweight. I folded my note tightly and wrote "Andrew" in script on the front. Then I made sure the hall was empty before I walked out of his office.

I was living with my best friend, Tami. We lived above an all-night diner and had plans to write a movie together. We were supposed to tell each other everything. That's what best friends do. But I didn't want to tell her about Andrew. I thought there was something ugly about it.

I had told her vaguely about having had an interesting conversation with an older professor at work who studied robots. She said he sounded cool. Then I told her I might get dinner with him sometime. She said that sounded creepy. So when I got home from work on Tuesday, I tried to get changed and out the door before Tami came home.

I put on my blue velour pants and picked out an eggshell-colored sweater that clung to my chest. My father had never seen me developed. The summer he died I was still confused and embarrassed by my new tufts of hair and the sour smell in my armpits. Now I stared at my reflection in the mirror. The whole thing didn't make much more sense to me at twenty-one.

The door opened as I was putting on eye shadow.

"I got all the leftover pastries," Tami said. She worked at

a coffee shop. That's where our movie would probably take place, so we thought of it as a research position. She looked at me. "What are you doing, Abby?"

"I told you. I'm having dinner with that professor guy."

"You said you *might* go out *sometime*. You didn't say you *were* going out."

"It's nothing big."

"It's a date."

"It is not."

"Then why are you wearing eye shadow?"

"I'm starting a new habit."

"It's a date, Abby."

"It's not a date. It's a Tuesday night."

Her voice got high and loud: "He's thirty years older than you. He could be your dad."

I got even louder: "Shut up! We're just going to have duck."

Andrew picked me up in his navy blue Saab. It had leather seats with coils that warmed you in the winter. He asked if I was warm enough, and I said yes. He dodged every pothole, swinging through a series of turns with only one palm on the wheel. We stopped at a light. He turned and looked at me. I did a fake sneeze to avoid making eye contact.

"You look sensational," he hollered over the classical music. He patted my knee. It didn't matter that it was a Tuesday night. This was a date.

We arrived at Andrew's building and got in the elevator. There were mirrors on all sides, so I decided to look at my feet. Andrew lived on the fourteenth floor in a beautiful apartment with tulips rising from tall, clear vases and the lights of the city blinking through the windows. Everything was on but turned down low, so the violins playing and the duck sizzling and the tulips tuliping would all mind their own business while we got to know each other.

I hopped up on one of his marble counters as those cute girls do in sitcoms. Andrew handed me a cracker with Brie on it. He lifted it to my lips and leaned in so close that my breath got caught under my ribs. I didn't want him that close, so I shoved the cracker into my mouth and said, "Mmmm. So what are we having besides duck?" Pieces of cracker flew out of my mouth.

Andrew laughed. "You'll see." He kissed my neck quickly. Then he went back to stirring something in a pot.

We had slim glasses of chilled white wine, and I stayed on the counter while Andrew cooked. I watched the back of his neck where his dark hair faded into his pink skin. He turned around and had me taste the orange-honey glaze. His eyes focused on my mouth as my lips covered the spoon, and I knew we were here in this moment for completely different reasons. I vowed to eat dinner and then ask him to take me home.

We had duck with steamed broccoli and creamy risotto that melted on my tongue. We talked about artificial intelligence and the role of pattern recognition in early education. When I stood up to clear the table, the floor wobbled. I concentrated on walking carefully to the sink and started rinsing off the dishes. That had always been my job at home. But Andrew shut off the water and asked me if I wanted dessert.

He had an espresso machine and said he wanted to show off. So I said I'd take a cappuccino, and then I excused myself to go to the bathroom.

I looked at the girl in the mirror and said, "Calm down. I'm going home."

Then I heard Andrew: "Come here! I want you to hear this CD."

He wasn't making coffee after all. He was in the bedroom, lying on the bed. He'd taken his shoes off and wore tan old-man's socks that were embroidered with tiny golf clubs. He was looking at the ceiling and listening to something so sad on his stereo. It sounded like a cello crying.

"Schumann wrote this for his wife before he went mad," he said. Then he held out his hand.

I stayed in the doorway. "I need to go home now."

"Really?"

"Yes."

"I promise I'll take you home," he said. "Just listen to this one piece."

He waited for me to take his hand. I did.

I lay on the bed next to him; he put his arm over me and we sort of spooned. He had a gray comforter. He was a gray comforter. He was my father. And we listened to that piece Schumann wrote for his wife. The whole thing. I loved being pressed into that moment, with his breath tickling my ear, still sweet with wine and orange and honey. I stared out his window at the lights from the downtown YMCA and I tried to hear only that moaning cello and to see only the light and dark of the night sky.

When the music stopped, Andrew whispered into my hair, "What do you want to do now?"

I wanted to have him hold me and count all the faces in the moon. Or tell me the story of how I first learned to use chopsticks when we ate noodle soup at Rockefeller Center. I closed my eyes and imagined him sitting in his maroon easy chair, his potbelly almost touching his knee. I listened for his *boom-skedada-boom-skedada* one-man jazz band.

But that moment had already happened ten years before. And Andrew didn't have my dad's potbelly and didn't smell like cocktail onions and Tums, and I wasn't his little girl, and this wasn't my home.

I was twenty-one years old. Not a little girl at all.

So I said, "Please take me home now."

I felt him sigh as he rolled away from me and put his feet on the floor.

"Okey-doke," he said. He stood up and turned his stereo off. There was nothing more to say.

And so Andrew took me home.

Abby Sher is a writer and performer living with her family in Maplewood, New Jersey. Her next book, Miss You Love You Hate You Bye, *will come out in February 2020. This essay appeared in January 2006.*

NO? NO? NO? LET ME READ BETWEEN THE LINES

STEVE FRIEDMAN

SHE DUMPED ME. WHAT'S IMPORTANT ARE NOT the details but the pronoun placement, she preceding me. But there is no villain here. My therapist suggests I repeat this mantra to myself. So I do. *THERE IS NO VILLAIN HERE.*

There is no green-eyed, wasp-waisted, pillow-breasted, sneering-queen-of-the-damned villain who dumped me so swiftly and with such imperious, frigid beauty that I experienced chest pains and shortness of breath, leading to something called a Cardiolyte stress test, which I've just discovered my insurance company may not pay for and which has left me not only miserable and lonely and occasionally sobbing in public bathrooms but also about six thousand dollars in debt. But no one is to blame here. My therapist suggests I repeat this phrase, too. *No one is to blame here.*

Did she have her reasons? Could I have been a better boyfriend? Is it telling that I was forty-eight when we met and never married, that I had spent the better part of three decades shedding wedding-happy sweethearts as a tailback dances away from fiendish linebackers, and that I had recently looked in the mirror and seen, staring back, male-pattern baldness and the egregious folly of my broken-field-running brand of romance? No good can come from dwelling on such questions.

So let's assume she had her reasons. What's important is not what she did or why. What's important is how I handled it. Personal setbacks and romantic rejection, according to authorities ranging from the Dalai Lama to the editors of *CosmoGirl,* offer us all opportunities to behave with grace and courage and self-respect. They also offer the opportunity to do what I did.

First, a day after she dumped me, I sent an e-mail message. An affectionate, graceful nondesperate note of about two hundred words that I worked on for three hours.

"I remember how wonderful and sweet things felt with you," I wrote.

That was good, I thought. Bold yet sensitive.

"From laughing and kissing on the tennis court to drifting in the ocean to holding each other and feeling so lucky and grateful. I just wanted to let you know that."

Not bad. Heartfelt but not clinging.

"And I wanted to own up to the toxic stuff I brought to the relationship. And to tell you how much you meant/mean to me, and to acknowledge the enormous amount of effort and kindness and love you brought to me and to our relationship."

I wanted her back so bad it gave me a stomachache. But I remembered with distress the times she had accused me of whining. I struggled over the last line for twenty minutes. I decided on "Write back if you want, but you don't need to feel obliged."

She didn't feel obliged. Which made me want to call her. Which made me want to have sex with her. Which made me want to wake up next to her, to grow old with her. Or to see her age and grow fat and ugly very quickly.

"She's dead to me," I told my friends. "I was mentally ill to have dated her," I told my friends. "Obviously a borderline personality," I told my friends.

"Why did I throw away the best thing I ever had?" I wrote in my journal. "Please, God, bring her back."

A week later I received an e-mail message. She thanked me for mine, apologized for not getting back to me sooner, admitted she was sad about how things had ended. Then came the key line: "I just hope we can have some sort of friendship going forward."

I decided this was her way of widening the dialogue. I decided this was her way of signaling that she was open to romance. I decided to ignore the advice of every single one of my friends. Not to mention my therapist. I telephoned her and suggested we try again.

She laughed. I persisted. She might have used the phrase "just friends," but I have not been able to locate those words in the detailed notes I kept of our conversation. Besides, are the details really that important? Didn't the fact that we had loved each other unconditionally and fully and intensely for four weeks and three days and nine hours and twenty-six and a half minutes mean more than mere words?

We made a date to see a movie. On the afternoon of, she canceled, pleading fatigue and an impending sore throat. She said she would rather make it another night. Was that okay?

But of course it was okay. I'm an adult, after all, not a child. *I am not a child.* She couldn't possibly suspect that I would be bothered by a postponed date, could she? Or hurt, suspicious, or deeply wounded, or reminded with a throbbing emptiness in my gut and sticking pain behind my eyes that when we were making out on tennis courts and drifting in ocean currents and discussing plans to hike in New Zealand together and holding each other in bed, nothing like a sore throat—excuse me, an *impending* sore throat— would ever keep us apart.

Feel better, I offered majestically. Call or write when you're on the mend and we'll celebrate your return to health, I suggested, manfully, powerfully. With confidence. No neediness there. No rage. No desperate, Cardiolyte-test-inducing words.

Almost a week later, on my birthday, as I was finishing a magazine profile, I received another e-mail note:

Hope you're having a v. special day!
Is the story done??
xoxo

I spent that afternoon and evening deconstructing the text. Two lines—not good. Eleven words on my birthday— not good. The "v." instead of *very*—not so good. But perhaps I was misreading. Perhaps I was bringing my own insecurities to bear on a sweet, loving signal from cyberspace. I cross-referenced her word usage with all her other e-mails which I had saved in a special file, and made a startling discovery. She had used the v. abbreviation before! Obviously it was a literary affectation or just a communicative tic. I had been entirely too eager to see in it proof of withered feelings. And it would be blind, and horribly unfair, would it not, to ignore the "xoxo," a clear, unambiguous indication that she was ready to drift with me in the ocean currents again?

I called her to clear things up. I didn't want to misunderstand her, I said. Did she want to date or not?

She suggested I not call again.

Oh yeah? Well then, I suggested *she* not call again. And that she lose my e-mail address. And furthermore, if she ever saw me on the street, she had better . . .

She hung up.

I stewed. I composed bitter letters about how she was incapable of love, how she didn't recognize the gifts I had given her. I did not send the letters. (Thank you, ten years of therapy.) I did not technically stalk her. I did ride my bike by her apartment building one evening, but I didn't stay for any legally significant amount of time. I drifted through the photos of her in my computerized slideshow, accompanied by Rebecca Luker singing "Till There Was You" over and over and over again. I lost ten pounds in two weeks.

Then, a blinding epiphany. I shouldn't have snapped at her on the phone. Of course she had recoiled. Who wouldn't? With the insight came a great sense of calm. With the calm, a sense of hope. With the hope, a plan. If I made her understand how much I loved her, how I in no way blamed her, and how I had changed and was now neither needy nor angry, but just a man filled with love and affection and magnificent intentions, then she might take me back, and we could get back to the ocean currents and tennis courts.

This time I stayed away from the phone. Spoken language was so easily misconstrued.

"I'm sorry," I wrote. "I'm really, really sorry." Then, I elaborated. "You have no idea how sorry I am." Other literary high points included: "I was such an idiot. You don't know how much I miss you. I wish you'd give us another chance, on whatever terms you want."

A week later she wrote back. She appreciated the apology. She didn't trust me. She wished me well.

Didn't trust me? No *wonder* she didn't want us to travel to New Zealand together. Surely if she knew about the chest pains and shortness of breath, her doubts about my sincerity would vanish. Surely if I told her about the way I listened to *The Music Man* while mooning over her digital photos, she would come back.

So I did. I told her. One more e-mail message. I told her all that. I also cited lines from *Casablanca* and *Malcolm in the Middle*. I mentioned my prayers.

That was almost a month ago. In that time I have reflected on and marveled at the chilly and dignified silence that has been maintained by the women I myself have dumped over the years. I have thought of the pathetic old professor in *The Blue Angel,* whom Marlene Dietrich compels to cluck like a chicken, of the poor bastard in *Endless Love,* of every mopey mope whom Frank Sinatra immortalized in his greatest loser anthems. I have considered the

Dalai Lama and the *CosmoGirl* way of life, and realized that I behaved with all the dignity of a furious and heartsick and grievously wronged Teletubby.

But I'm getting better and, finally, getting it. I know this because two weeks ago, for the first time in a long time, when a woman smiled in my direction on the subway, possibilities occurred to me. I know this because, for the first time in a long time, I'm not racing to check my e-mail every day or gazing at photos of her.

I haven't destroyed those photos, or the letters and e-mails, as friends have advised. But I don't need to. This time she's really dead to me. Really. I mean it.

Steve Friedman is the author of The Agony of Victory, Driving Lessons, *and* Lost on Treasure Island *and the co-author of two* New York Times *bestsellers. He lives in New York City and can be found at stevefriedman.net. This essay, the first "Modern Love" column, appeared at the end of October 2004.*

DURING A NIGHT OF CASUAL SEX, URGENT MESSAGES GO UNANSWERED

ANDREW RANNELLS

I DON'T REMEMBER HIS LAST NAME. HIS FIRST NAME was Brad, which is the perfect name for a relatively face-less memory from your early twenties. He was handsome, with a nice smile and startlingly blue eyes.

I had always thought that when the eyes got too blue it looked like a person had no soul. You're seeing too deeply into their head, and there's nothing back there. But I had never dated anyone with blue eyes, and it was springtime. Brad also had a nice body, muscled, but with extremely soft skin. And the sex was good, I think.

There is a great debate among straight women and gay men as to what counts as sex. Most of my female friends think oral sex doesn't count. I disagree. I count it all. If someone has an orgasm, I count it. My female friends also hold a deeper misunderstanding that anal sex, for gay men, is like a handshake. News flash, ladies: Sometimes we don't want to do it with our dates just as much as you don't want to do it with yours.

This was only my second date with Brad. We didn't know each other well. We never would. His haircut was fussy and his hands were a little feminine, but his cologne was appealing. I was twenty-two and hadn't been on many dates, so this was one of my first forays into courtship. A bonus: He lived just blocks away from me in Astoria.

If you have ever lived in Astoria, Queens, you know that getting people to go there at the end of the night is like asking a stranger for a ride to the airport. Brad was going to do for now. I was young and dating and independent, and I had highlights in my hair.

The conversation at dinner was dull but he laughed at almost everything I said, so for a comedy narcissist like me, he was an ideal companion. As we ate, my Nokia flip phone started ringing. It was my sister, Julie.

I declined the call. My phone was new and I was still getting used to it. I didn't love that people could reach me whenever they wanted. I preferred calling my answering service, which made me feel like an old-time movie star. My father had shown me Doris Day movies when I was young, and she was always checking her service for messages from suitors or Hollywood producers.

After dinner we went to a gay bar packed with other gay people on dates, because what's more fun than trying not to look like you're checking out other people while learning about your date's siblings?

Brad and I drank our Cosmos (it was 2001, and if Carrie

Bradshaw was doing it, so was I) until his eyes looked less soulless and we started kissing.

My phone vibrated again. Different sister. Becky. I ignored it.

Another round, more making out, another call, Julie again. My drunkenness, mixed with my desire to be present for Brad, made the calls easy to dismiss. Our making out turned a corner—we were now prone on a banquette—and I had just enough sense left to suggest a cab.

Feeling like a high roller, I offered to pay. En route to Astoria there was more groping, more kissing, more picturing him as Paul Walker. At my apartment we went straight to the bedroom. It lasted longer than it needed to. And then there was the cuddling and holding and sweating and panic and the falling asleep next to a basic stranger and waking up and thinking: *Do I like this? Does he like this?*

I excused myself to use the bathroom and opened my phone again. Six more missed calls. My stomach dropped. I was now sober enough to know that something was very wrong.

I started listening. Julie was in hysterics. Something about my dad falling and an ambulance. In the next message, Becky was calmer but shaken. A heart attack or stroke, they weren't sure. Next: My mom telling me not to panic. Next: Julie telling me to panic.

I skipped to the last message, from Doug, my kind-of brother-in-law (they hadn't married), from just fifteen minutes earlier.

I called; he answered immediately.

During my niece's first birthday party, my dad had

collapsed after handing off the hamburgers he had been grilling. The party was at my parents' house, though my dad wasn't living there. My parents were divorcing and my father, at sixty-one, had moved into a depressing bachelor pad near his office.

The last time I was home, a month earlier, I had visited him with my youngest sister, Natalie. The walls were beige and so was the carpet. The furniture he had picked out was too large and too dark. The place was filled with stuff, yet looked empty.

He was trying to make it a home but didn't know how. I went into his bathroom to cry. I didn't want him to see me feeling sorry for him. He didn't belong there; he belonged in his home.

I pulled myself together, and we ate sandwiches. He put out the plates and napkins and a canister of Pringles. When he opened his kitchen cupboard, I saw that it was stocked with canned stew. I had to clench my jaw to keep from crying again.

After dinner we watched TV.

"I want you to feel at home here," he told us.

"I should stay here the next time I visit," I said, which seemed to make him happy.

When Natalie and I left, my dad was standing at the top of the stairs. I turned and yelled up, "I love you, Dad." It was the last thing I said to him.

"I love you, Andy."

And that was it.

Doug had tried to do CPR. The paramedics had used the paddles to get a weak pulse. Now my father was in a coma.

I imagined the scene: the party decorations, the yard

full of toys, the deck where he fell, the potted plants my mom put out every spring, my mom crying, my sisters crying, the uneaten hamburgers, the little girl's birthday cake.

It was all too much. I started to cry. Loudly.

Brad came out to see what was wrong. His hair was mussed and he was completely nude. He stood in front of me, his semi-erect penis at eye level, while I tried to get more information from Doug: What hospital? Should I get on a plane?

I gestured for Brad to sit down. He started rubbing my back, which felt like torture. I was embarrassed about crying in front of him but didn't care enough to stop.

After I hung up, he tried to hug me. "What happened?"

I wanted to shout: *Clearly nothing good! Put on some pants!* Instead, I tried to explain.

As Brad paced the apartment, still naked, suggesting plans of action, I felt a growing sense of disgust. I didn't even like this guy. Why did I have sex with him? Everything seemed wrong. The apartment seemed cramped and dirty. I hated everything inside of it. I caught myself in the mirror and cringed at my dyed blond hair. Why did I do that to myself? I looked like a fool.

I told Brad he should go, that I needed to make some calls. He sat and put his arm around me. "You shouldn't be alone right now," he said, kissing my neck.

I leaned into him. I didn't want to be alone. I didn't want to be where I was. Everything felt off. Is this how my father felt in that sad apartment? Like everything was off?

I kissed Brad lightly. "I really need you to leave."

He looked hurt, but he stood up when I did. Then he hugged me for way too long.

"OK!" I said. "Goodbye!" I walked into the bathroom and locked the door. I stared out the window listening to him get dressed. Then I heard the front door shut. He was finally gone.

Within a few days, my father was gone, too.

Over the following months, Brad sent me text messages and a voice mail message that went unanswered. I had too much to sort out. And I was embarrassed, I suppose.

About two years later, Brad walked past me on Ninth Avenue. We almost stopped but only nodded at each other, smiled awkwardly, and kept going. I felt like I owed him an explanation, some ending to our story, but I just couldn't do it. I had to keep moving forward.

I had straightened out much of what felt so wrong that night. I now had a job I was proud of, an apartment I was proud of. I had buried my father and in doing so had buried that whole chapter of my life. Which meant there could be no Brad, no trace of that time, of that night.

It wasn't generous of me, or kind, but that's what I did. Most important, I never got highlights again.

Andrew Rannells is an actor and writer in New York City who published his first book, Too Much Is Not Enough, *in March 2019. This essay appeared in July 2017.*

FOR BEST HOOKUP RESULTS, USE YOUR WORDS, OK?

GABRIELLE ULUBAY

I HAD INVITED HIM OVER ONLY FOR SEX, SO WHEN I woke the next morning to the sight of him putting on his pants, I said, "Do you need me to walk you out?"

"No, I'm just going to use the bathroom," he said. "I'd like to stay, if that's OK."

And it was. So he stayed for the rest of the day, never more than a few inches from me. We left the room only to use the bathroom or to shuffle to the kitchen for snacks. Meanwhile, my roommates laughed, gossiping about my "sexcapade with the cute guy from Tinder."

"I think you're the girl of my dreams," he said. "I can't believe we met on Tinder."

I had never been the girl of anyone's dreams—not even my own. I always imagined the quintessential girl of men's dreams to be taller than me, thinner, more poised, and blond.

But my lover insisted, and we lounged on top of each other until late in the afternoon.

Later, I said, "Do you usually have sex with girls the night you meet them?"

He cocked an eyebrow. "Why, do I come off as a slut?"

I laughed nervously. "Of course not."

Finally, he answered: "Not really, no. I mean, I wouldn't turn sex down, but I wouldn't go looking for it, either."

After a minute, I asked, "Do I come off as a slut?"

His voice softened. He wrapped his arms tighter around me. "No, not at all. You actually come off as a lady."

Maybe he wanted it to sound like a compliment, but my doubts about his sincerity made it feel more like a blow. I wondered if he was lying to make me feel better or to ensure more sex later.

As a child, I was always told, "Use your words"—shorthand for saying precisely what I mean and what I expect from people. As an adult, I've noticed that a lot of people aren't very good at using their words, especially before and after hookups. Few ever seem to say precisely what they mean or what they expect.

Regardless, I smiled and said, "Really? Thank you." I kissed him on the cheek, the temple, the forehead. "And you come off as a gentleman."

And he did. But I secretly hoped that he was the same as me, that his chest also simmered with hidden indiscretions, and that the speed with which we slept together was as typical for him as it was for me. Because if it wasn't, I would have to wonder if, upon discovering the truth, he would recoil. I would have to wonder if he would think of me as dirty or morally deficient, even though he already said he found me gentle.

"Wow, you've got a beautiful smile," he said, idly stroking my waist, my stomach, my hips, my thighs. "You're really the full package."

"You don't have to say that."

"I know I don't," he said. "But I mean it."

He told me I was smart, funny, creative. "You've got good karma, Gab," he said.

I said, "You see things in me I didn't know were visible."

I don't know why I fell for it, especially when I hadn't even gone looking for it. For some reason I've always been susceptible to thinking my life would be vastly improved by the solution to a single problem. In high school, I thought, *It will all get better when the braces come off* or *when my skin clears up* or *when I go to college.*

And now, older and supposedly wiser, I find myself thinking it will all get better when I find romance. When I have a man who wants me despite how fallible, loud, or political I can be. Someone who, with a kiss, can snap me out of my self-pitying reverie. I think about how long I've been ready to find the beauty in another human being, to caress the scars of someone as flawed as me and to feel that person reciprocate.

That night I hadn't been looking for romance, but my two-time lover embedded himself in my consciousness when he told me I was the girl of his dreams, and I can't help but think how cruel that was, considering how it all turned out. Our goodbye was a kiss on the mouth and a wink as he stepped off the subway.

He had grinned and said, "I'll see you later," but he never saw me again. I have since learned that *later* means the same thing it did when I was a child and wanted to do something extravagant: It means *I don't want to* or *If I feel like it*.

Now I'm told, "You only like him because he flattered you," and "Good sex can trick you into thinking you like anyone."

"What did you expect, Gab?" my friend said. "You can't form a connection with somebody that fast."

I shrugged. "I didn't mean to. This felt different."

She sighed. "Your problem is that you jump into things too quickly."

"OK . . ."

I thought there must be something terribly, medically wrong with me if I could so badly misinterpret a situation. I wanted to see a doctor. I wanted a diagnosis. I wanted to ask my lover if he had found himself disappointed, if I wasn't who he wanted me to be.

My friends tell me I need to love myself. I'm told this will make my life better, much in the way braces and clear skin were supposed to make me beautiful. When I ask how to do this, my friends become philosophers and say, "You need to find it within yourself." Their advice is so abstract that I wonder if they, too, have searched and cannot find it.

How do I search within myself? I imagine reaching down my throat and rummaging until I find some bright little mass labeled "self-love." It has been hiding, perhaps behind some bothersome organ or within the folds of a stubborn muscle. And when I find this magical panacea, I will say, "Oh, there you are. Where have you been all this time?" And I will set it back inside of me, this time in the correct place.

My question is: How will I know when I have found this thing that I never realized I lost, and what will happen when I do?

But I don't really think my problem is a lack of self-love. I enjoy sex for its own sake every bit as much as a man does, and I'm honest about that. What confuses matters is all this sweet talk, followed by the vanishing act.

"Ghosting is the most cowardly way to end a relationship," I once said to a male friend in a room with a guy who had ghosted me years before.

"Would you really rather someone tell you to your face that they don't have feelings for you?" my friend said.

"I'd rather have that than be made to feel like an idiot," I said.

Not too long after, a man I slept with told me I was beautiful while we were walking to my apartment in the middle of the night. He caressed the back of my hand with his thumb and smiled, but it meant nothing—under the orange glow of streetlights, I knew, even broken glass looks stunning.

"I feel so lucky right now," he said. "I can't believe a girl like you would give me the time of day."

I texted him the next week, but he never responded. Annoyed, I noted that I wouldn't even have thought to text him if he hadn't blanketed me with such gratuitous flattery.

And then my two-time lover called me a lady. He added me on Facebook and told me to keep in touch. He said my skin was soft and my smile was beautiful and he couldn't believe he had found someone like me.

He said, "I'm never mean to girls."

I smiled. "So you're a self-proclaimed nice guy?"

"Yes. What's wrong with that?"

"Nothing," I said, draping my leg over both of his. He slid his arm beneath my head like a pillow. "But I don't want a guy to be nice to me just because he feels obligated to, you know? I want him to be nice because he means it."

"That makes sense," he said, tangling a hand in my hair and kissing me on the forehead.

I don't wander into casual sex expecting it to yield a relationship. I have never understood why some guys seem to think flattery is the key to a bedroom they've already been welcomed into. They say they would love to date me and then wonder why, the next day, I think they want to date me.

I neither require the flattery nor deserve the ghosting. With hookups there's no need to be mean—just say what you mean. Use your words.

Gabrielle Ulubay is finishing a master's degree at University College Cork in Cork, Ireland. In addition to the Times, *she has published pieces in* Film Ireland, O'Bheal, *and* Alma *and with Trinity College Dublin. This essay appeared in January 2018.*

I THINK I LOVE YOU

WHEN CUPID IS A PRYING JOURNALIST

DEBORAH COPAKEN

M Y INTERVIEW WITH JUSTIN MCLEOD WAS WIND-ing down when I tossed out one last question: "Have you ever been in love?"

The baby-faced chief executive had designed Hinge, which was a new dating app. My question was an obvious throwaway.

Justin looked stricken. No one, he said, had ever asked him that in an interview. "Yes," he finally answered. "But I didn't realize it until it was too late." Then he asked me to turn off my recorder. I hit Stop.

Off the record, he looked relieved to unburden himself. Her name was Kate. They were college sweethearts. He kept breaking her heart. (Tears now swelled in his eyes.) He wasn't the best version of himself back then. He had since made amends to everyone, including Kate. But she was now living abroad, engaged to someone else.

"Does she know you still love her?" I asked.

"No," he said. "She's been engaged for two years now."

"Two years?" I said. "Why?"

"I don't know."

I was by then a year into a separation from a two-decade marriage. I had been doing a lot of thinking about the nature of love, its rarity. The reason I was interviewing Justin, in fact, was that his app had helped facilitate a post-separation blind date, my first ever, with an artist for whom I had fallen at first sight.

That had never happened to me, the at-first-sight part. He was also the first man to pop up on my screen after I downloaded Justin's app.

For those keeping score at home, those are a lot of firsts: first dating app, first man on my screen, first blind date, first love at first sight. I was interested in understanding the app's algorithm, how it had come about, how it had guessed, by virtue of our shared Facebook friends, that this particular man, a sculptor with a focus on the nexus between libidinal imagery and blossoms, would take root in my heart.

"You have to tell her," I said to Justin. "Listen—" And I told him the story of the boy I had loved just before meeting my husband.

He was a senior in college, studying Shakespeare abroad. I was a twenty-two-year-old war photographer based in Paris. We had met on a beach in the Caribbean, then I visited him in London, shell-shocked, after having covered the end of the Soviet-Afghan war.

I thought of him every day I was covering that war. When I was sleeping in caves, so sick from dysentery and an

infected shrapnel wound on my hand that I had to be trans-
ported out of the Hindu Kush by Doctors Without Borders,
my love for him is what kept me going.

But a few weeks after my trip to London, he stood me up.
He said he would visit me at my apartment in Paris one
weekend and never showed. Or so I thought.

Two decades later, I learned that he actually had flown to
Paris that weekend but had lost the piece of paper with my
address and phone number. I was unlisted. He had no answering machine. We had no friends in common. He wound
up staying in a hostel, and I wound up marrying and having
three children with the next man I dated. And so life goes.

By the time Google was invented, the first photo of me
to appear on his screen was of my children and me from an
article someone had written about my first book, a memoir
of my years as a war photographer. Soon after, he married
and had three children with the next woman he dated. And
so life goes.

I found him by accident, doing research on theater com-
panies for my last novel. There he was above his too-
common name. I composed the email: "Are you the same
man who stood me up in Paris?"

That's how I learned what had happened that weekend
and began to digest the full impact of our missed connection.

His work brought him to New York a few months later,
and we met for a springtime lunch on a bench in Central Park.
I was so flummoxed, I kicked over my lemonade and dropped
my egg salad sandwich: Our long-lost love was still there.

In fact, the closure provided by our reunion and the
shock of recognition of a still-extant love that had been de-
prived of sun and water would thereafter affect both of

our marriages, albeit in different ways. He realized how much he needed to work on tending to his marriage. I realized I had given mine all the nutrients and care I could—twenty-three years of tilling that soil—but the field was fallow.

Hearing of Justin's love for Kate while seated on another New York City bench four years later, I felt a fresh urgency. "If you still love her," I told him, "and she's not yet married, you have to tell her. Now. You don't want to wake up in twenty years and regret your silence. But you can't do it by email or Facebook. You actually have to show up in person and be willing to have the door slammed in your face."

He laughed wistfully: "I can't do that. It's too late."

Three months later, he emailed an invitation to lunch. The article I wrote about him and his company, in which he had allowed me to mention Kate (whom I had called his "Rosebud"), had generated interest in his app, and he wanted to thank me.

On the appointed day, I showed up at the restaurant and found the hostess. "Justin McLeod, table for two," I said.

"No," he said, suddenly behind me. "For three."

"Three? Who's joining us?"

"She is," he said, pointing to a wisp of a woman rushing past the restaurant's window, a blur of pink coat, her strawberry blond hair trailing behind her.

"What the—? Is that Rosebud?"

"Yes."

Kate burst in and embraced me in a hug. Up close she resembled another Kate—Hepburn, who had appeared in the comedies of remarriage I had studied in college with Stanley Cavell.

These films, precursors to today's rom-coms, were made in America in the 1930s and '40s, when showing adultery or illicit sex wasn't allowed. To pass the censors, the plots were the same: A married couple divorced, flirted with others, then remarried. The lesson? Sometimes you have to lose love to refind it, and a return to the green world is the key to reblossoming.

"This is all because of you," Kate said, crying. "Thank you."

Now Justin and I were tearing up, too, to the point where the other diners were staring at us, confused.

After we sat down, they told me the story of their reunion, finishing each other's sentences as if they had been married for years. One day, after a chance run-in with a friend of Kate's, Justin texted Kate to arrange a phone conversation, then booked a transatlantic flight to see her without warning. He called her from his hotel room, asked if he could stop by. She was to be married in a month, but three days later, she moved out of the apartment she had been sharing with her fiancé.

I felt a pang of guilt. The poor man!

It was OK, she said. Their relationship had been troubled for years. She had been trying to figure out a way to postpone or cancel the wedding, but the invitations had already been sent, the hall and caterer booked, and she didn't know how to resolve her ambivalence without disappointing everyone.

Justin had arrived at her door at nearly the last moment he could have spoken up or forever held his peace. By the time of our lunch, the two were already living together.

Soon afterward, I had them over for dinner to introduce

them to the blossom-obsessed artist who bore half of the responsibility for their reunion. He and I hadn't worked out as a couple, much to my pain and chagrin, but we had found our way back into a close friendship and even an artistic collaboration after he texted me a doodle he'd been drawing.

In fact, we had just signed a contract to produce three books together: *The ABC's of Adulthood*, *The ABC's of Parenthood*, and—oh, the irony—*The ABC's of Love*.

"What was the doodle?" Kate asked.

I showed her the drawing on my iPhone.

"Are those ovaries?" she asked, smiling.

"Or seeds," I said. "Or flower buds, depending on how you look at it."

All perfectly reasonable interpretations of love begetting love begetting love, which is why we were all gathered around my table that night, weren't we? Because real love, once blossomed, never disappears. It may get lost with a piece of paper, or transform into art, books, or children, or trigger another couple's union while failing to cement your own.

But it's always there, lying in wait for a ray of sun, pushing through thawing soil, insisting upon its rightful existence in our hearts and on earth.

Deborah Copaken is the New York Times *bestselling author of* Shutterbabe *and* The Red Book, *a columnist at* The Atlantic, *and a staff writer on Darren Star's new show,* Emily in Paris. *Her memoir,* Ladyparts, *will be published by Penguin Random House in 2021. She splits her time between Brooklyn and Los Angeles. This essay appeared in November 2015.*

SLEEPING WITH THE GUITAR PLAYER

JEAN HANFF KORELITZ

IN THE AGES OF MAN, THERE ARE THE CLASSICS—
infancy, childhood, adulthood. We have the midlife crisis,
of course, so dear to therapists and second wives everywhere. There is adolescence, which in some men seems to
last . . . oh, well, when does it end? But in the last few years
I've experienced, via my husband, another masculine stage,
one I'd been blissfully unaware of. This is the time of a
man's life that I must now and forever think of as the guitar-
in-the-basement phase.

Six years ago, when my husband, Paul Muldoon, a poet
who teaches at Princeton, brought home an electric guitar,
carried it down to the basement of our house in New Jersey,
and plugged it in, I was laughing too hard to absorb the
enormousness of what was happening. I knew he loved
music. Growing up in Ireland during the 1960s, he was
present at the birth of British rock, and he knew far more

about American blues and its influence on both sides of the Atlantic than I had ever cared to learn. He leaped into action when U2 tickets went on sale and had dragged me, over the years, to many, many concerts I despised. (I once fell asleep listening to Bob Dylan at the Beacon Theatre.)

Still, I failed to realize that the very loud sounds coming from beneath the living room floor portended great changes for our family. I was pregnant with our second child at the time, and to be honest, I wasn't focusing very well. When Paul played his guitar in the basement, the whole building vibrated, and I would sit there, one story up, swaying with nausea. When I couldn't stand it any longer, I went to the top of the basement stairs and flicked the light to get his attention. "Please. Stop." He stopped. But not for long.

This was not, I would soon discover, a mere matter of purchasing a single musical instrument. We were on an acquisition conveyor belt of more guitars and related equipment, the charms of each soon negated by the undulations of the next. After that first guitar, a Cort, and its sidekick amplifier, Paul ordered up a Fender Stratocaster, a Gibson Les Paul, a Marshall amp, a reissue of a 1952 Telecaster ("like the guitar Keith plays"), an Ibanez acoustic/electric, and a Fender Acoustasonic amp.

It was a new and unwelcome side of a man I thought I'd known pretty well, a man who never shopped, who wore a watch with a cracked plastic band, and who drove an old unlovely car, knocked askew by a deer a decade ago. Now he was making special trips to Sam Ash in New York City. (I imagined the salesmen nudging one another, "Here comes another guitar-in-the-basement dude, dude.") It was getting crowded down there under the floorboards.

Gradually, I began to understand that it wasn't just about my husband. There were hordes of men out there, roughly his age, frolicking in guitar wonderlands and shoring up amp arsenals in their own basements. In the weeks after September 11, when I began each sad day with the "Portraits of Grief" in the *New York Times,* I read again and again of men commuting home from their working lives, descending their basement stairs, and rocking their Jersey or Westchester or Long Island houses to the rafters.

Once, at a friend's dinner party, Paul was seated next to a terribly dull financial manager I'd been shackled with during cocktails. To my surprise, they quickly began an avid conversation, which lasted all through the meal. I kept my eye on them, at a loss to imagine what they might possibly have found to talk about, let alone with such animation. "He has a Stratocaster in his basement," Paul said happily as we drove home. "He just got a wah-wah pedal."

Inevitably, Paul started to play with some of these men. There was a lawyer who possessed an entire recording studio in his apartment, then a professor of Renaissance poetry with a vast collection of guitars. Initially, heading out after dinner with a guitar packed into the backseat was a grand occasion, a thrilling adventure for him, if not for me, but soon it became a more routine outing. "You don't mind if I rehearse tonight, do you?" he'd ask. Rehearse? I'd think, baffled. He was still learning basic chords on the instrument. Rehearse?

It took a long time for me to figure out what I was dealing with. But I'm a woman, which means that, in my heart of hearts, I have long understood that certain things are never going to happen in my life. I won't, by way of example, be modeling swimsuits for *Sports Illustrated,* representing my country as an Olympic gymnast, or dancing Coppélia for the New York City Ballet.

I have dealt with these disappointments and, in the idiom of our age, moved on. But my husband—my wonderful, endearing husband, who is extremely successful at writing and teaching poetry—believed, at the age of fifty-three, that it was utterly possible for him to become a rock guitarist. On a stage. In front of an audience.

Our twelve-year-old daughter dubbed the new band Freaks with Guitars, but the actual name encompassed more subtle humor. They were called Rackett, and by now the three older men had been joined by three cute young guys, just out of college. They started writing songs: the Renaissance poetry professor on music, my husband on lyrics.

A couple of those cute young guys could really sing. The Renaissance poetry professor was a superb guitar player, actually. Within months, the recordings made in the lawyer's studio were sounding not all that different from the music my twelve-year-old was blasting in her room. The keyboardist, who runs his own breath-mint company, began to talk about producing the eventual CDs.

I no longer bothered to try to talk some sense into my husband. What sense, after all? My notion of reality had departed the day I came home to find Paul playing, over and over, a recorded phone message from one of the few rock stars we both revered, Warren Zevon. Mr. Zevon had read some of his poetry. When Paul hit Play on the answering machine, I heard the author of "Werewolves of London" and "Excitable Boy" pronounce my husband "The best damn poet on the planet."

In due course they would meet, become friends, and write two songs together, including "My Ride's Here," the title track of Mr. Zevon's penultimate album. Books about the music business began to accumulate in our bathroom. Paul formed a publishing company to register his lyrics and became a member of ASCAP. Copies of *Spin* and *Guitar World* began to arrive monthly, along with an inexhaustible supply of Sam Ash catalogs. Rackett was offered its first gig, in a Greenwich Village club. The band's catalog of original songs stretched to thirty, then fifty. Bruce Springsteen produced a live recording of "My Ride's Here" for Warren Zevon's posthumous tribute album.

I refuse to conclude from all this that I have been unknowingly married to a rock star for nigh on eighteen years. I simply could not have been that unobservant, failing to notice the spandex in the closet, the tour bus in the garage, the groupies at the mailbox. Nor is this a story about years of hard work, prodigious innate musical talent, and patient honing of "craft" reaching their inevitable, just conclusion.

It occurs to me that much of his success in this odd endeavor derives from the fact that he just didn't know the whole thing was impossible, that his dearth of musicality, advanced age, and lack of rock star lips meant that it was flatly impossible for him to become the thing he had decided he wanted to become. Then again, some of that obtuseness might have derived from being male in the first place.

Unlike women, for whom menopause serves as an unignorable transition, a line dividing one part of life from another, men have no midlife marker to brake before, or even to steer around, in the hinterland from their youth to their age; there is only a great, elastic middle. Is it any wonder they lose track of where they are, and think they can do anything? And evidence being what it is, I'm forced to concur. Should Paul waltz in tomorrow and announce that he has decided to become an engineer, a painter, or a matinee idol, I'm afraid I will be forced to give him the benefit of the doubt.

Onstage, he looks like a middle-aged Irish poet, bespectacled, dressed in the same rumpled suit he teaches in. He is not a great musician and still can play only seven chords (which is four more than you need, he points out). But to succeed at anything is just so unlikely in the first place. Why should the fact that he's fifty-three and a musical neophyte make watching his band rock out onstage any more bizarre for me? Why should I be so surprised by the possibility of being surprised?

Then again, one of the great pleasures of being shocked by some amazing thing a loved one does is being aftershocked by something in ourselves. I'll admit that I have now done things I never thought I'd do, like bounce up and down in the dark basement of a rock club with a host of twentysomethings, an activity that might have recalled my lost youth had I ever done it when I myself was a twentysomething. I have seen things I never thought I'd see, like a group of college students raising a sign with Paul's name on it in the audience at a Rackett performance.

And I have said something I never thought I'd say, at the stage door of a New York club, as I attempted to carry his guitar—one of his guitars!—downstairs to the dressing room. The bouncer, after giving me a very dubious look, wondering, perhaps, if I hadn't just wandered in off a New Jersey soccer field (which was precisely where I'd been a few hours earlier), asked if he could help me.

"That's all right," I told him, hoisting the guitar. "I'm with the band."

Jean Hanff Korelitz is the author of six novels, including Admission, You Should Have Known *(coming to HBO as* The Undoing)*, and* The Devil and Webster*, and the co-adaptor/ co-producer of* The Dead, 1904*, an immersive adaptation of James Joyce's* The Dead*, presented by the Irish Repertory Theatre (www.thedead1904.com). She lives in New York City with her husband, Paul Muldoon, who is now in a band called Rogue Oliphant. This essay appeared in March 2005.*

HEAR THAT WEDDING MARCH OFTEN ENOUGH, YOU FALL IN STEP

LARRY SMITH

YES, WE WERE ON AN IDYLLIC ROCK ON A postcard-worthy cove on the New England coast. Okay, I did have a ring—seven actually, none with diamonds. Fine, there was fumbling and nervousness and the oh-so-slyly stashed champagne in the vegetable drawer in the refrigerator back in the cottage. But let's get one thing straight: I didn't say the words. I didn't need to ask. She didn't need to answer. It never mattered.

Will you marry me? Who wants to know? Who cares? Not me. Not her. Is there anyone else, really, whose opinion counts?

We'd been together seven years. What with medical advancements, free-range chicken, and Pilates classes, I estimated we were good for fifty, maybe sixty more. We didn't need a piece of paper to make what we had more real. What we needed was to learn Spanish and surf in Costa Rica. We

needed to buy an apartment together and discuss light fix-
tures. Maybe we even needed to breed. We didn't need to
get married.

This troubled the usual suspects (grandparents, mothers). But it also, to our surprise, concerned those we expected to embrace our "unconventional" lifestyle (the pierced,
the gay, the younger siblings). At a coleslaw-wrestling con-
test in Daytona, Florida, a grizzled biker told her she was
nuts ("What are you doing with this guy? He got money?")
and called me an idiot for not sealing the deal ("You better
hold on tight, boy, before someone takes her away").

What, exactly, was the problem? We didn't have one.

This wasn't a political statement. We'd been to twenty-
seven weddings—twenty-seven!—in our seven years together.
We'd made toasts, danced with stray cousins, coaxed extra
bottles of booze from busboys. No one could accuse us of
not supporting, with gusto, this hallowed tradition.

This wasn't the fallout of family trauma. My folks are
high school sweethearts, married forty years, for better, for
worse. Her parents divorced when she was in high school—
not ideal, but not exactly unusual for someone born in 1969,
nor, in her case, the cause of large therapy bills later.

This wasn't even a hipster, postmodern, too-cool-for-
school stance. Despite a popular misconception, there was
never a time when I thought getting married was a sellout
to convention. In fact, I always assumed I would get married.

She'd tell you her dream as a young girl never involved a
man whooshing her off her feet, shoving a rock on her finger, and sending her down the aisle. She'd tell you she's
always been tough-minded and independent—and never ex-

pected to be in a relationship this long. She'd tell you the whole thing has been a pleasant surprise, that she's shocked it's working out this well. I saw no reason to rock this boat.

Cut to the night before our wedding: let's call it May 2006. A cool breeze greets the guests at the rehearsal dinner in a funky café in Key West. The mixing and mingling subsides as a playful pastiche of our previous separate lives is projected at the front of the room. Roll video.

Mine comes on first. The *Dennis the Menace* youth. Inappropriate uses of the high school PA system that would make the Desperate Housewives blush. Kooky Atlantic City summers at my grandmother's house and staying out all hours with a series of playthings she and her best friend Bunny Bookbinder didn't approve of. A theme emerges: girls. He loves them. Short, tall, big, small. White, black, Asian. Older, younger. Laurence David Smith is girl crazy. What's more, he himself is no big deal to look at, so he's got to work harder. But he loves it. Look at him chase! Why give this up? Ever? Now we see him in his mid-thirties, living in New York—best place on earth for a decent-looking dude with a good job and no discernible drug or anger-management problems to become acquainted with a lot of women. He could go on like this for years—five! ten!—before settling down with a choice woman in his target demographic. Fun!

Her life story is the real crowd-pleaser, though. Here she is, being conceived by hippie parents, San Francisco, 1969. The brief but memorable child-modeling career. The slow, sure birth of a stubborn independent streak and indifference to boys during high school. The years at an all-women's college. Jobs at rollicking bars. Exploits in Indonesia. Dangerous love. Make no mistake, she's the one always being chased (and rarely caught) in this movie. Theme: don't fence me in. Marriage? Don't bet your lunch money on it.

The man who loves women and the woman who won't be corralled—makes for great video. You say: Tigers never change their stripes. We say: We're together, we're happy. Survey says: If it ain't broke, don't marry it.

What happened?

I'm not entirely sure. My path to carrying seven gold rings (one for each year we'd been together) in a hermetically sealed bag as I cautiously kayaked out to that rock was subtle, a combination of personal outlook, impossible-to-define emotional pull, and gut instinct that even now I am still piecing together.

There was never a tipping point, no eureka moment when I realized that doing the most traditional thing possible was a good idea. Some guys say they know immediately She's the One. Not me. Whether it's a sweater or software, it takes some time for me to know if I want to keep something, one reason I always save receipts. I can't say there was an instance when I looked into the pale blue eyes of the girl I met over corned beef hash at a café in San Francisco and thought, *This is it.*

Now, after eight years, I know. When did I know? Was it how she helped me deal with the death of my grandfather? The relief I felt when she finally answered her cell on September 11? That great hike in Point Reyes? Because she cried when the Sox finally won? The way my nephew greets her like a rock star when she walks into the room? Perhaps I should have known right from the start, that morning of our cross-country trip, when she required one last trip to

Arthur Bryant's for a half slab of ribs for breakfast (and ten minutes into the meal saying to me, "Hey, baby, why don't you pop open a beer?"). Or did I not truly know until seven years later when we found ourselves forced apart for more than a year? Who can say? It's the big moments, maybe, but it's the little moments as much or even more.

I do know one thing: those twenty-seven weddings had a lot to do with it. They were joyous, righteous, nup-tastic affairs (as Woody Allen said about orgasms, "the worst one was right on the money"). The idea of putting our own personal stamp on a tradition we've now seen take so many shapes and forms—including but not limited to full Masses, lobster bakes, white doves, exploding chupahs, gigantic soap bubbles, freezing-cold skinny-dipping, and one quasi-orgy—has become more appealing, not less, with each one.

But that's the party, and there's never been any doubt that we'd know how to throw a grand one to celebrate our staying power. Getting married—with the blood tests and stamped reply cards and tax benefits—is much more than that.

Like I said, I always thought I'd get married, until I started realizing maybe I wouldn't, or at least didn't have to. I've had long-term relationships before and exactly zero pressure to pop the question. No one has cared less than my fiancée, which makes her Woman of the Year to my buddies who are feeling the heat from partners who want to see a tangible, sparkly finish line. And although I'm also crazy about her unflappable strength and independence, I see the self-doubting downside: Does this person really need me? Does she wear her steely self-sufficiency like a badge of honor that will be stripped away if some priest, judge, or ordained-for-a-day pal of ours starts yammering about the power of unions?

So I figured that one out (she needs me, duh; and anyone who has watched us interact knows how much I need her). And I figured the rest of it out by the way she pinches the skin of my elbow during the bride's father's *we-cannot-be-hearing-this* toast. I figured it out from the little squeeze of my hand during a beautiful ceremony, and her quiet tears landing on both our fingers. And I figured it out from the ever-so-slightly different look I saw in her eyes the last time a perfect stranger questioned my sanity for not locking this lady up. And slowly as ever, yet indeed as sure as it gets, it dawned on me—she *wants* to get married. And I want to get married. To her. There's nothing less original than marriage—this is perhaps the least original idea I've had in a long time—but I needed to get there myself, on my own terms. And after all these years (so many that people have long stopped asking), one thing I actually had going for me was the element of surprise.

So what the hell, let's do it. I still don't believe marriage is the only path to happiness or completeness as a person, but it's the right thing for us. So I asked her. Or, more accurately, what I said, sitting next to her on that silly island in a scene straight out of *Brides* magazine, was something about love and commitment and not going anywhere and here are these rings I got you, and if you want to actually make it official, that's cool, and if you don't, that's cool, too. And if you want to have a wedding, I'm into it, and if you don't, who needs it. She's still unclear what it was I was asking, exactly, but when she got done laughing, she said yes. And then she threw off her clothes and jumped in the water.

My friends joke that I've been to twenty-seven wed-dings and now it's finally time for one funeral . . . for my singlehood. Which is sad like any funeral, sure, but this death is no tragic accident. I look at it more like euthanasia I'm performing on myself, a mercy killing.

I'm ready, babe. Pull the plug.

Larry Smith is the creator of the Six-Word Memoir® project and book series, which most recently published the collection Six Words Fresh Off the Boat: Stories of Immigration, Identity, and Coming to America. *He lives in Columbus, Ohio. This essay appeared in December 2004.*

THE RACE GROWS SWEETER NEAR ITS FINAL LAP

EVE PELL

SAM AND I DATED FOR TWO YEARS. THEN, WHEN I turned seventy and he eighty, we had a joint 150th birthday party and announced our engagement. We married a year later.

We came from very different backgrounds. Sam, a Japanese American who had been interned in the camps during World War II, worked his way through college and was happily married to his Japanese American wife for more than forty years until her death. I grew up as a fox-hunting debutante whose colonial New York ancestors were lords of the manor of Pelham. Typical of my much-married family, I had been divorced twice.

We belonged to the same San Francisco–area running club. He was a rarity—a charming, fit, single man of seventy-seven. I wanted to get to know him better.

I devised a plan. Our mutual friend Janet had in her

house a small movie theater that seated about a dozen people; she often had parties there. I called her. "This is very
seventh grade," I began. "But I'd like you to invite Sam
to one of your screenings. I'll come to any movie he's coming to."

Soon after, she called. "He's coming on Thursday."

There were eight or ten of us there that evening. After
the movie, as we were all standing around and chatting,
someone mentioned *The Motorcycle Diaries*, a new film
about Che Guevara.

"I'd like to see that," I said.

"I would, too," Sam said. Short pause. I held my breath.
He looked at me. "Would you like to go?"

Squelching the urge to high-five Janet, I said yes. We set
a date for the following week; he'd meet me at the theater.
But when the day came, our movie was sold out.

What to do? We looked at what else was playing and
chose *Sideways*. I have only a vague memory of some plot
about men and wine, but a sharp memory of sitting next to
Sam. And when *Sideways* was over, we decided that since
we hadn't met our objective, we'd see *The Motorcycle Diaries* another day.

Sam and I began running together. Early on, however, I
was faced with a dilemma. At a half marathon in Humboldt
County, he went out fast and was way ahead. But as the
miles went by, I crept closer and closer and I could see, from
the way he was running, that I had more energy left. What
to do? Should I beat him and risk his being resentful? Some
men really hate being bested by a woman.

I could slow down and let him beat me, but that would
be patronizing to him and make me resentful. Then I thought,

If he gets annoyed that I ran faster, he's not the man for me. So I sped up, patted him on the behind, and said, "Come on!" I ran on to the finish and, as it happened, he couldn't keep up. But I needn't have worried. Sam didn't get upset—in fact, he seemed pleased I had run well. And so we grew together.

Sam and I often ate at Chinese restaurants where I received some fortune cookies that truly lived up to their name. Two of my favorites:

Persevere with your plans and you will marry your love.

Stop searching forever. Happiness is just next to you.

One evening at the movies, after we had been seeing each other for several weeks, I felt his hand on mine. If I close my eyes and concentrate, I can recapture the moment: the dark of the theater, the warmth of his hand, my happiness. One might not expect an old grandmother to feel a surge of romance, but I did, and I knew that his reaching out was a brave gesture. I reciprocated, inviting him in for tea when he took me home. I have a narrow, uncomfortable sofa in my living room, poorly designed for intimacy, but nevertheless that was where we sat, and that was where we kissed before he went home.

There was a complication: I could feel that Sam was conflicted about our budding relationship because of his loyalty to his wife, Betty, who had died six years before. In my younger years I would have felt competitive, as if his love for her meant less for me. Now I knew differently, and one night I spoke my mind.

"I know that you loved Betty very much, and I have great respect for your marriage," I began.

"But I think you have room in your heart for me, too."

He hugged me and went home.

Several days later he asked, "Are you going to run the 5K in Carmel next week?"

"Yes."

"Would you like to go together?"

"Yes." I had no idea what he had in mind, but that became clear a few days later. We were talking after a run; Sam looked bashfully down at his shoes as he said: "I have made a reservation in Carmel for a room with one bed. Is that OK?" It was.

I realized that the last time he had been dating was in the early 1950s, before his marriage, and he had entirely missed the change in customs of the '60s and '70s. When he began staying over at my house, he always stopped the newspaper at his house so the neighbors wouldn't know what was going on. But for all his adherence to decorum, he was a true romantic.

A few months later, when we were both in Europe on separate trips, we met in Barcelona. This was a leap. Traveling together in a foreign country would be a more exacting test of our relationship than our jaunts to movies and races. But in this, as in almost everything else, Sam was perfect. When I arrived at our hotel, he was there with wine, chocolates, and flowers. For all our anxiety about traveling together, we meshed. On the flight home, Sam declared, "We must never travel separately again."

From then on, we were well and truly together. We had few outside pressures: He was retired with a comfortable pension; I was a freelance writer with an outside income; our middle-aged children were on their own. We had nothing to do but love each other and be happy. Sam and I did things younger people do—we ran and raced, we fell in love and traveled and remodeled a house and got married.

After the ceremony, we flew to Hawaii. "You must never call this a honeymoon," he told me. "That way no one can ever say that the honeymoon is over."

We traveled to Italy to compete in the 2007 World Masters Athletics Championships (what I fondly call "The Geriatric Olympics"), where we both won gold medals in our respective age brackets: 70 to 74 for me and 80 to 84 for Sam. At home, we planted a garden; I finished writing a memoir. Every morning we did push-ups; every evening we sat on the rim of our bathtub and flossed our teeth. He called me "sweetheart." He never forgot an anniversary, including our first movie date. I gave him flowers on Betty's birthday.

Old love is different. In our seventies and eighties, we had been through enough of life's ups and downs to know who we were, and we had learned to compromise. We knew something about death because we had seen loved ones die. The finish line was drawing closer. Why not have one last blossoming of the heart?

I was no longer so pretty, but I was not so neurotic either. I had survived loss and mistakes and ill-considered decisions; if this relationship failed, I'd survive that too. And unlike other men I'd been with, Sam was a grown-up, unafraid of intimacy, who joyfully explored what life had to offer. We followed our hearts and gambled, and for a few years we had a bit of heaven on earth.

Then one day the tear duct in Sam's right eye didn't work, and soon his eye began to bulge. One misdiagnosis and failed treatment followed another until there was a biopsy. A week later his doctor called to say Sam had stage four cancer that he would not survive.

There was the agony of Sam's fight to live, which he waged with grace and courage. Desperate to lessen his suffering, I learned to give hospital nurses $20 Starbucks cards to get special care for him. Every day I brought him bowls of his favorite watermelon balls. But one morning he couldn't eat even those, and a few hours later he died.

Not only was I happy during my short years with Sam, I knew I was happy. I had one of the most precious blessings available to human beings—real love. I went for it and found it.

I yearn desperately for Sam. But the current pain is very worth it. He and I often told each other, "We are so lucky." And we were. Young love, even for old people, can be surprisingly bountiful.

Eve Pell is a writer and runner who lives in Mill Valley, California. This essay appeared in January 2013.

LOVED AND LOST? IT'S OK, ESPECIALLY IF YOU WIN

VERONICA CHAMBERS

DATING FOR ME WAS ALWAYS LIKE THAT VIDEO game: you try to follow the dance moves, and the further you get in the game, the trickier the moves become, until you are just a flailing mess. I was clingy and desperate and wore my heart on my sleeve, falling madly in love repeatedly, only to meet with heartbreaking rejection at every turn.

Which is why it is nothing short of a miracle that two years ago I was swiftly and happily married.

Until then I was a case study in *He's Just Not That Into You,* or so I've been told. I haven't read that book: friends warned me that it would trigger too many unpleasant memories. Apparently it is all about women like me: women who wear blinders about the men in their lives, who come on too strong and fall in love with the wrong people over and over.

I'm sure there are many of you out there. And if you're

one of us, here's what I have to tell you, what I wish someone at some point had told me: It's okay.

It's okay to fall deeply for one loser after another. It's okay to show up at a guy's house with a dozen roses and declare your undying affection. It's okay to have too much to drink and call your ex twenty times and then to be mortally embarrassed when you realize your number must have shown up on his caller ID. It's okay to stand at a phone booth in Times Square on New Year's Eve, drenched like a sewer cat in the pouring rain, crying your eyes out because the man you are infatuated with has decided that he needs some space.

It's okay because I believe that all of these grand gestures and heroic attempts to follow E. M. Forster's simple advice to "only connect" are not really about this guy or that guy. Making a fool of yourself for love is ultimately about you, about how much you have to give and the distances you will travel to keep your heart wide open when everything around you makes you feel like slamming it shut and soldering it closed.

Not to digress into too much pop psychology, but I sometimes think that I never had a chance at being one of those girls who could play it cool. My parents' marriage was a soap opera saga of dramatic exits and mind games and affairs. When I was little, my father would force me to choose which parent I loved more. If I chose my mother, he would react with fury. If I chose him, he would smother me with hugs and kisses, luxuriating in his victory, then promise to come back for me soon.

Soon could mean two days or two weeks or two months.

I learned early on that love meant never having to follow through on your promises.

My mother, bless her heart, tried to keep me from becoming a desperate girl with a daddy complex. In seventh grade, I got my first boyfriend: one very handsome junior high school star athlete named Chuck Douglas. We went to different schools, so our relationship consisted of long, meandering phone calls, most of which were initiated by me.

One day, when my mother could not reach me after school for three hours straight, she came home early with the intention of beating some sense into me. When she found me sprawled underneath the dining table, the phone cord wrapped like a bracelet (or a handcuff) around my arm, she took pity. She led me into her bedroom and asked me how often I called Chuck.

"All the time."

"And how often does he call you?" she asked.

I shrugged.

"You can't chase boys," she said. "They don't like it."

I was thirteen. Chuck Douglas was dating me, a certified nerd, in a sea of buxom cheerleaders. My mother's words meant nothing. I was already lost to the cause.

In college, I discovered women's studies and somehow managed to wrap the words of Gloria Steinem and Angela Davis neatly around my now well-solidified boy craziness. "I'm a feminist," I declared. "I don't need to wait for a man to ask me out."

So I asked out guy after guy after guy: the very epitome of "he's just not that into you." I dated numerous gay men who hadn't yet come out. It became a kind of service after a while, coaching ex-boyfriends out of the closet. I went out with a techno DJ who invited me to go sailing with his parents. I hated his taste in music, and he was a terrible kisser, but I still cried a week later when he dumped me.

In my twenties I had two long-term relationships that nevertheless ended, and I found myself back out in the wilds of the dating world. At this time the hot self-help dating book was *The Rules*. There were many rules that were supposed to help you lasso a man, but the one I remember said that you should never accept a date for Saturday after Thursday.

The Rules reminded me of that conversation I had with my mother about the swoon-worthy Chuck Douglas. I understood that the rules were good for me, but so is tofu, and I just can't stand the stuff.

My friend Cassandra insisted that men are like lions; they want to chase their prey. She suggested that I smile at a guy I was interested in instead of barreling him over with conversation. "See what he does," she said. "If you're feeling playful, then maybe give him a little wink."

Soon after, I was invited by a friend to take a trip to South Africa. One enchanted morning my friend and I were having breakfast in the hotel restaurant. Across the room I spied a charming man with the kind of friendly face that you feel you have known forever. Leaving the restaurant, I stood up and saw that he was looking my way. I smiled. He smiled back. Feeling bold, I winked, then tripped on a step and fell on my face.

The next few minutes were dizzying as I was surrounded by hotel staff offering me ice and bandages. Then I heard a voice amid the cacophony; it was the man I had winked at. I turned away, mortified.

"You should see a doctor," he said.

I insisted that I was fine.

"Well, let me be the judge of that, because I happen to be a doctor."

He took me out to dinner that night and every night for the rest of my trip. We exchanged phone numbers, and even though I lived in New York and he lived in Sydney, Australia, I called and called him because I was so sure that what I felt for this man was, if not love, then certainly magic.

It wasn't. To give the guy a little credit, we lived continents apart. Even if he was that into me, it would've been a hard row to hoe.

It was about this time, when I was in my late twenties, that I read a nugget of advice, probably in a women's magazine, that I took to heart. This article suggested that if you knew you were going to meet the love of your life in one year, you would really enjoy this year. This seemed reasonable.

So while I still tended to wear my heart on my sleeve and to commit too quickly, I also had some really fun one-off dates with guys I knew were never going to call. I went to the theater and to hip-hop shows and tried to relax about the whole dating and mating thing.

About a year later I met the man who would become my husband. The friend who kept reintroducing us insisted that, unlike the vast majority of men I was meeting in New York, Jason was a guy who could hold his own. He was not a *Sex and the City* Mr. Big, a type I was well acquainted with: the übersuccessful guy who keeps you at arm's length. Nor was he a starving artist who was willing to fall in love while nursing commitment issues about things like holding down a job and paying bills.

Jason was a regular guy: he had a good job, owned a house, liked his parents. Eight months after our first date he proposed.

Suddenly the role I had been playing my entire dating life was reversed: I didn't want to get married. I'd never been angling for a ring. What I had wanted all through my twenties was a really great boyfriend: someone who called when he said he would, who would get up early and go running with me over the Brooklyn Bridge, and who would jump at the chance at weekend getaways in the Berkshires.

I wanted someone with whom I could read the Sunday paper in bed, who would sit next to me during foreign movies, who would bring me chicken soup when I felt ill, who would send me flowers on Valentine's Day, and sometimes for no reason at all.

Jason said he wanted all the same things, too. But to him the relationship I described was marriage, not dating.

So I said yes.

Which is probably why after two years of holy matrimony I still make the mistake of calling Jason my boyfriend. He is in every way the best boyfriend I've ever had. No one ever told me that a really great marriage can make up for two decades of horrible dating. No one ever said that all those guys who were just not that into you can be, for women, the psychological equivalent of notches on a bedpost.

I'm happy now that I dated the DJ, the doctor, the candlestick maker. When I look back at those relationships, I can see that in the midst of all the drama I managed to have a goodly amount of fun.

What would have happened if any of those relationships had lasted, bumbling along in all their glaring wrongness? Instead of just being dumped and consoling myself with pints of Chunky Monkey and viewings of *Breakfast at Tiffany's,* I could have been facing any one of these men in divorce court, or being forced to see them every Saturday afternoon, when we met to swap custody of our children or our cocker spaniel.

Thankfully, all those men were just not that into me. They did me a bigger favor than I could ever have known.

Veronica Chambers is an editor at the New York Times *and the editor of* Queen Bey: Celebrating the Power and Creativity of Beyoncé Knowles-Carter. *She's still happy all those guys weren't that into her. In the words of Beyoncé: "Boy, Bye." This essay appeared in February 2006.*

SINGLE, AND SURROUNDED BY A WALL OF MEN

SUSAN M. GELLES

SOMETIMES I PLAY A KIND OF SHIVERY GAME IN which I think about how different my life would be if I had made other choices. One thing leads to an unforeseeable other.

After spending my twenties as a would-be musician, I attended law school in New York City. I graduated owing about $100,000 in student loans. Luckily, I found a job at a terrific but demanding law firm, where I was assigned to share an office with an associate named Daniel.

Daniel and I bonded as soldiers who share a trench during wartime do. We were both shy, but working together on days, nights, and weekends has a way of breaking down reserve. He would send me fake emails from terrifying law partners, and I'd jump out of empty offices and startle him.

We had no romantic connection, but we talked each other through our relationship messes. We agreed that so-

cializing in unstructured settings was particularly fright-
ening. Thus, we hid in our office and avoided the firm's
weekly cocktail hour. The prospect of schmoozing with unfamiliar co-workers put us both in a defensive crouch.

But even the best of wartime alliances eventually weaken.
After three years, Daniel left the firm and moved to another
city. It took me another two years to pay off my loans. About
five seconds later I fled the battlefield and joined the legal
department of a slower-paced publishing company.

With more free time, I gathered my courage and signed
up for a singles event run by a group that held regular mix-
ers. I was thirty-seven, at my life's midpoint, and it looked
like a dull, downward slide from where I stood. So I squashed
my misgivings and showed up at the next mixer.

It had nine attendees—five men and three other women
besides me. We each spoke about ourselves into a microphone. Then came the part I always hated: the mingling.
The event's organizer gave the usual admonishments. None
of us were to be rude. If someone approached us, we should
talk to them for at least a minute.

Chairs scraped and we rose. I spotted an attractive guy
and approached him. He beamed, came toward me, and
then swerved to speak with the woman he really had in
mind. I saw a second guy and scooted over.

"Hi there!" I said.

"Sorry," he replied, and kept walking.

I left, vowing never to attend a singles mixer again. I
emailed Daniel, who wrote back that the same group was
sponsoring another mixer in a month, and I should go. *Ha
ha*, I thought. I began to research single-parent adoption
and signed a contract for a small co-op apartment.

One Friday afternoon some weeks later, I was sitting at my desk at my blessedly quiet job. Here no one urgently needed a memo summarizing legal research. No one expected me to work that night. This was peacetime lawyering.

I decided to clean out my email inbox. And there it was: Daniel's email about the singles mixer. The event would start at six that very evening in Midtown Manhattan.

I was dressed in a flannel shirt, jeans, and sneakers. But what did it matter? I wouldn't meet anyone. And who needed love anyway? Then again, maybe it would be fun. But wouldn't I have to talk to people? *I can leave at any time*, I reminded myself.

This mixer had about eighty attendees, who sat on chairs in the meeting room of a high school. It took an hour to pass around the microphone. I scribbled notes of what certain men said about themselves: This one was a contractor who liked Shakespeare, that one was a lawyer who liked opera.

Then came the dreaded mingling. An angry-looking man stomped over and demanded to know how I was doing. Moments later, another man, this one with a fixed grin, asked what kind of movies I liked.

The mingling was to last for thirty minutes, but I couldn't pretend to be perky and relaxed for that long. If I didn't leave soon, I'd start telling inappropriate personal stories, such as the one about the nun in elementary school who told me I'd never amount to anything because I spoke so softly. After I chatted with a few more men, none of whom interested me, I hurried out to the bathroom and locked myself in a stall.

Why was I putting myself through this again? It was exhausting. Maybe love was overrated. Maybe love was just what people claimed to feel for anyone who'd put up with them. I leaned against the wall and closed my eyes. I could hear the chatter of women, turning on faucets, flushing toilets. *I'll just wait here*, I thought, *until the mingling is over. Then I'll go back and see if anyone has written down my ID number as someone they'd like to date.*

I returned to the meeting room, only to discover that the mingling session wasn't quite done. Immediately the lawyer who liked opera positioned himself in front of me. He was immaculately dressed in a suit, his dark hair clipped short, his brown eyes penetrating. Meanwhile, I could have played the part of the stablehand who groomed his horse.

"Hi!" I said. "I remember you. You're a lawyer."

"Yes," he said, and his face remained a closed door.

"I'm a lawyer, too. I used to be a litigator. Now I'm in-house at a publishing company. What kind of law do you practice?"

"Real estate," he said flatly.

"Ah. And you like opera. What period do you most like, or what composer?"

His expression eased just a bit. "I like Puccini."

A dim memory came to me of sitting in a music library a decade earlier, listening to an opera that I thought was terrible. "I remember listening to *Tosca* once, years ago," I said. "It was so overblown."

A rather long pause ensued. Somewhere behind the lawyer, organizers urged people to take their seats.

"*Tosca* is my favorite opera," the lawyer said.

It was all so deliciously awful: the mingling, how I was dressed, the futility of trying to meet anyone. Even when I tried to show interest in a person, I unwittingly flung an insult instead.

I couldn't help it: I laughed. "I'm sorry," I said. "It was probably a scratchy recording. Or I was in a grumpy mood that afternoon."

"No doubt," the lawyer said.

All of us took our seats, dutifully wrote down the ID numbers of people we liked, and handed in our scorecards. Then we waited for the computer to sort the results.

I matched with the lawyer, whose name was Richard. A week later, we enjoyed a nice dinner at an Italian restaurant. Richard wore another impeccable suit, and I wore a dress. I asked him, "If you hadn't talked with me during the mingling session, would you still have written down my ID number?"

"Oh, no," he said. "I would never date someone I hadn't at least spoken with first." He tilted his head, remembering. "It was hard to get to you that evening."

Yes, I thought, *because I was hiding in the bathroom.*

"You were surrounded by men," he continued.

You poor deluded one, I thought.

"I had to get through a wall of men," he said.

I decided to opt for honesty. "There was no wall of men."

"Yes," he insisted, "there was!"

"I was hiding in the bathroom," I said.

"There was a wall of men."

That's probably the beginning of love: when you see someone in a way that defies reality, but which makes perfect sense to you.

On our second date, we went to the Metropolitan Opera and saw *Tosca*. We emerged with the throngs into a crisp autumn night. The side streets were almost empty, though, and the two of us strolled along, talking excitedly about how evil Scarpia was, and the terrible fate that befell Cavaradossi.

"It's nice of you to forgive me for insulting your favorite opera," I said.

Richard gave an amiable shrug. "At least you'd heard of it."

As we walked, we held hands and talked about musicals. Somehow we found ourselves back by the now-deserted fountain in front of the opera house. It was midnight.

"Sing something by Rodgers and Hart," I said.

Richard considered. "I'm wild again," he sang. "Beguiled again. A simpering, whimpering child again."

Two years later, we married. More than a decade after that, we're the parents of ten-year-old twin boys.

When I ask myself how I managed to get so lucky, I think: Because my life in music didn't work out. Because I went to an expensive law school even though I had no money. Because I needed a well-paying job. Because the law firm assigned me Daniel as an officemate. Because Daniel sent me that email reminder.

But most crucial, I think, is that I stopped hiding in the bathroom before it was too late.

Susan M. Gelles is a writer who lives with her family in Larchmont, New York. Her essay appeared in December 2015.

WHEN EVE AND EVE BIT THE APPLE

KRISTEN SCHAROLD

WHEN YOU ARE RAISED TO BE A GOOD CHRIS-tian girl, you don't just go to church; you date the church. Church is the significant other with whom you spend weekends and evenings, the boyfriend whose friends become your friends, the girlfriend with whom you share all your dreams.

I was a really good Christian girl, so I didn't just date the church; I married it.

After graduating from a Midwestern college whose motto is "For Christ and His Kingdom," I moved to New York City. It was my first time out of the evangelical cocoon, and my priority was finding a church I could love, commit my life to, and make my spiritual and social center.

My search ended in Brooklyn, where I found a church of young creative people and fledgling professionals who, like

me, were looking for a faith less burdened by fundamental-
ism. We forged a quick camaraderie, including with our
pastor, who was as much friend and peer as spiritual leader.
We hung out in the pews on Sundays, but also in bars and
each other's living rooms throughout the week.

Soon this congregation became my beloved. I took my
membership vows and began leading a Bible study, teaching
Sunday school, attending weekly planning meetings, and
signing up for countless other duties. I committed to this
church with the vigor and joy of a new bride.

Like most single women in my position, my next priority
was finding a husband in this church. There is a motif of
love triangles in Christianity. Like the love of the Father,
the Son, and the Holy Spirit, Evangelicalism 101 also teaches
the holy trinity of matrimony: man, woman, church. So I
scanned the pews each week looking for someone with an
unadorned ring finger.

One Sunday, I noticed a new woman in a suede jacket,
her short dark hair tucked under a brimmed hat. Our conversation was unremarkable, and yet I was captivated. I
tossed out the most evangelical invite: "Do you want to
come to my Bible study?"

She did. Then she came over for dinner. Then she began
sleeping on my couch. We met for coffee and whiskey and
eventually lost track of who paid for each other's tabs. I convinced her that biking in New York wasn't too hazardous, so
she bought a bicycle on Craigslist.

When she crashed—twice!—we went back to my apartment, where I cleaned pebbles out of her skin and bandaged
her ankle. Then we unknowingly went to a museum exhibi-

tion featuring gay and lesbian art, and I was forced to think about us. But I wouldn't let myself acknowledge what was so painfully obvious.

Over the following months, however, as Jess began stashing extra shoes in my closet and bringing home groceries to expand my diet of frozen burritos, I couldn't deny that I was falling in love. And with that realization, I fell off cloud nine and stared into the fires of hell.

I finally came out to myself. Then I scrambled right back in. At stake was my soul and identity, my entire worldview and spiritual cosmology, my relationships with friends, family, God. That holy trinity of husband, wife, and church haunted me even as it slipped out of reach.

It was a crisis of eternal proportions. I fell deep into an inferno of shame and panic. My fear of hell shut down any capacity to imagine a future with Jess. I repented of what Christians call my "struggle with same-sex attraction," but still I found incomparable delight in her. I read countless books on homosexuality, and yet clarity escaped me. Fighting for solace, I convinced myself that Jess and I were just friends.

That worked until one night when we went to the ballet, and I kissed her, and she told me she loved me. For the first time, I felt complete, loved, known. Lying beside her healed my past and present self. It also confirmed my worst fears. I woke up terrified. I needed to kick Jess out and end things with her immediately.

But first, we had to go to brunch. It was the kind of brunch we couldn't skip: a going-away celebration for a good friend.

We barely endured the long mimosas and eggs Benedicts as we contemplated our catastrophically changed lives à la Adam and Eve postfruit, full guilt. Finally, the check was squared, and we left to confront the reality of us.

As we walked, Jess noticed a distraught homeless man standing in traffic. Never one to ignore a person in need, she called him over to the sidewalk, where he began to share his story of the wounds life had inflicted upon him. Jess listened patiently. I stood aloof and awkward while she offered to buy him lunch.

When they exited a nearby bodega, the man had a bag of food, a hot coffee, and something like a smile on his face.

"How much?" the man asked.

"Oh, nothing. It's a gift."

"How much?" the man insisted.

"OK, well," Jess hesitated. "A dollar."

He reached into his jacket and pulled out a coin purse, counting out four quarters and placing them in Jess's hand. Then he left.

Jess looked at the quarters. "These are the most valuable things anyone has ever given me," she said. "I don't even know what to do with them."

For most of my life, I had been given a slew of definitions around love and relationships that were easy to verify with Scripture, just as a flat Earth was once confirmed by looking at the horizon. But watching Jess interact with this man, I saw a new horizon, one that was more complicated.

In Jess, I saw the love Jesus preached, one unconstrained by conditions and extended to everyone, especially the forgotten, the stranger. Jesus never mentioned homosexuality. His cosmology was not studded with creeds, crimes, and contempt; its essence was loving the marginalized. Every fiber of Jess's being reflected this. She embodied the attributes Jesus was most passionate about: compassion, kindness, justice. How could loving someone who loved so well be wrong?

I felt my cramped religious framework of false dichotomies and moral starkness beginning to collapse. What once seemed like a bleak choice between losing my soul or losing my most cherished friend was in fact a lesson that true love is the only thing that could save me.

There was still much turmoil ahead. Many people opposed our relationship and insisted that if we loved each other, we didn't love God. Our pastor was one. We had first gone to him to confess what we then considered our sinful relationship. But over time, we discussed our evolved thinking with him, hoping that our years of faithfully serving the church would be our witness, and that our pastor—a friend—would agree to disagree where our theology diverged.

Instead, he gave us an ultimatum: break up or lose our church memberships. Soon after, the church divorced us.

Looking back through that messy love triangle between Jess, our church, and me, I kept asking myself what Christ's love required, and the refrain I kept hearing was "love your neighbor as yourself." Jess didn't usher me into only true romantic love, but also true agape love, showing me that the most foundational precept is the trinity of loving God and your neighbor as you love yourself. We eventually found a new church that champions this belief and embraces all people. I now have the joy of serving as an elder there.

Two years after our first kiss, Jess and I sneaked onto an empty Rhode Island beach. Only a few stars and a cloudy moon illuminated our running and jumping as we let freedom eradicate our shame. As our eyes adjusted to the darkness, we saw a lifeguard tower and clambered up. With the ocean at our feet and the horizon at eye level, we sat side by side in the night air.

"Let's write something," Jess suggested, pulling out the journal we shared.

"No, let's just enjoy this," I insisted. The moment seemed perfect as is.

"Well, I'll write something, and we can read it later."

Jess scribbled and then handed me the open notebook, shining her phone's flashlight on it. The light was a shocking intrusion upon our private darkness, so I asked her to turn it off.

Instead, she pushed the journal into my hands. When I looked down, I saw a hole cut out in the middle of all the pages. Inside lay a ring.

My head spun. I waited for her to ask me those four fated words, but she was silent. The moment didn't need words.

I took the pen and wrote *yes* on the page.

She put the silver band on my finger and gave me a matching ring to place on hers. Then she asked if I remembered the homeless man we met that morning after brunch.

I laughed. "Of course! Why?"

"I figured out what to do with those quarters. They were melted into our rings. Fifty cents each."

Kristen Scharold is a writer in Brooklyn. Her essay appeared in November 2016.

WOULD MY HEART OUTRUN ITS PURSUER?

GARY PRESLEY

I AM NEAR QUADRIPLEGIC, A RESULT OF POLIO, and I cannot stand. I have limited strength in my arms, enough to function once I'm in my chair but not enough to get into or out of the chair.

To be able to live in my own apartment, as I desired, rather than in the custodial care of a nursing home, required the assistance of a rotating crew of attendants to transfer me from wheelchair to bed, bed to wheelchair, wheelchair to shower chair . . . you get the idea. Ten to twenty minutes in the mornings and in the evenings usually did the trick. Otherwise I went about my business, which included working at an insurance agency. No warehousing for me, thank you.

The female attendants preferred to come in pairs, all the better to help a man into his bed, and there undress him. I am somewhat deferential in the company of women, and I had made a conscientious effort to avoid any touch, any word that might be construed as improper. With that the arrangement sailed along with no problems, soon settling into a job done and forgotten—at least until Belinda, a young mother of two boys, showed up as half my attendant team. She was working evenings to pay for her college education.

Earlier that day I had noticed that part of the assembly of my shower chair was loose. "Do you know how to use a socket wrench?" I asked Belinda.

"Sure," she replied. "I was a tomboy. I helped my father all the time when I was a girl."

She had a silky sheet of straight brunette hair pulled together at the nape of her delicate neck, exotic dark hazel eyes, and a dancer's lithe body. She might have grown up a tomboy, but what I saw was a beautiful woman.

"There's a wrench set in the lower left drawer of my desk," I said. "Get it, and I'll show you how this thing goes back together."

As the days went by, Belinda sometimes began taking her turn on my transfer schedule without a co-lifter.

"Doesn't it bother you to come alone?" I asked.

"Why? I can outrun you."

And with that the necessity of my transfer faded into the background, and we began to talk about other things: books and films, my work and hers. It seemed a natural evolution that after a few weeks Belinda's routine occasionally included a friendly visit before she started her 3-to-11-p.m. shift.

One day she dropped by with her sons. "This is Matthew and Christopher," she said.

The boys spoke up, even though Matthew, the younger,

held tight to his mother's skirt. It was evident she had told them about my wheelchair. Matt was all red hair and freckles, while Chris carried his mother's brunette coloring.

And so it was that the man in a wheelchair, sardonic and standoffish, and the vibrant young woman who loved science and worried over how she would support her sons developed an odd connection, a link to a place where hands might touch, but thoughts and feelings and emotions began to flicker like lightning beyond the horizon.

I was past forty, my anger and frustration over being paralyzed mostly burned away. But it never occurred to me that the friendship, the connection, between Belinda and me might also be the bridge between caution and passion, between isolation and connection.

"I really don't see the chair," Belinda said a few months after we met. "I see you."

But I didn't believe her then. I had been paralyzed too young, when I was too callow, and in a time and place where most people with disabilities were seen as invalids and shut-ins, passively accepting limitations and retreating behind an accepting smile to avoid injury, neglect, abuse, or rejection.

Belinda was twenty-six, beginning study for a master's degree in microbiology, but she was also a single mother with minimal income. Nearly a decade had passed as she worked as a nurse's aide to pay for her classes and for day care for her sons. And her life was becoming more hectic as she undertook graduate studies.

I did not know how to love, not then, but I knew how to be a friend. I tried to help her with her boys, getting them ready for the bus when she had an early appointment, watching them after school and seeing that homework was done and bellies filled.

One late summer day Belinda asked me to accompany her to the nearby university city. "I need a man's opinion on what a professional woman should wear," she said. The master's program allowed her to supplement her income by working as a graduate teaching assistant. She was apprehensive about looking the part, and so we set out in my van.

On the way, as we passed a restored VW Beetle in the adjacent lane, she pointed to it and said, "One of these days, I'm going to find one of those and rebuild it."

Only half-listening, I murmured, "If wishes were horses, beggars would ride."

"What a mean thing to say," she snapped, turning away.

She was driving my van; I sat behind her with my wheelchair secured by tie-downs. "I'm sorry," I said automatically, but I didn't understand what caused her reaction. The sardonic aphorism made perfect sense to me; I was an expert on wishes.

"People have a right to dream," she said.

We were quiet as Belinda bought dresses. She liked floral prints. I liked a navy blue with tiny white polka dots. I bought lunch, and we drove to my apartment. As we waited for her boys' school bus to arrive, she sat on my couch, still subdued, her legs tucked under her, dark hair cascading down the side of her face. She gazed out the front window at the row of cedar trees along the driveway.

"I really didn't mean to hurt your feelings," I said.

"It's all right. I shouldn't be so sensitive." I could see her despair reflected in the slump of her shoulders.

I knew about despair. I wore it like a familiar coat, incapable of accepting what must be tolerated and petulantly ignoring what must be acknowledged. But at that moment—at the sight of such sadness in one usually so open and upbeat, sadness in the spirit of a woman who needed something from me—I wanted to offer more than mumbled words of apology. But I also knew that to push myself deeper into her world might carry us to a place where I might lose what I had made of myself, a place where I knew I could no longer hold tight to the hard reality that kept me sane.

I believed I did not deserve to love Belinda. I believed I should not allow her to love me. I held hard to the idea I should be content to ride out the remainder of my life without complaint, a burned-out case, an absurd hodgepodge of broken parts, a beggar who no longer wished for a horse. But she was also a woman, beautiful and vibrant, and I was a man—in a wheelchair, true—but a man full of heat and desire that sometimes rendered the chair irrelevant.

And I was the keeper of an obscene little secret I had known perhaps since I had been stuck in the iron lung, and surely from some vague moment later, the point where I realized I would never walk again. It is a thing that will sit rancid in my gut until the day I die, a thing that until then had eaten away at any illusion that love and marriage for me would be like it was in books or movies. And it was this: I would be physically dependent upon those who might love me. I am a chore, an obligation, and I will ever be so. I could not rationalize how a woman might love me and not soon come to hate the millstone I believed myself to be.

All this ricocheted through my mind—not in words but in a fog of melancholic unease—as I stared at Belinda. Suddenly, she moved from the couch and across the few steps between us. I opened my arms, and she dropped into my lap and put her head on my shoulder. There was no sound, no words between us, only her tears and my silent wonder.

Friends. Lovers. Perhaps that day was a hint that there might be a path through the thicket of my insecurities. I only remember the gift, the magic, the seamless transition from what I could never imagine into that which I will treasure until my last breath. A kiss. A touch. The sweet scent in the shadow of her neck.

"We should stop this, you know," I said, my mouth against her hair. "You need to find someone else."

"Where can I find a man silly enough to stay home with my boys when they have chicken pox?" she replied, smiling and lifting up to kiss the top of my head. "I like it that you put me first."

There was that, I suppose, but it seemed only natural, given that she couldn't miss her teaching assignment and I'd already had chicken pox as a child.

Months later, Belinda stopped by my apartment and held out a small box. Inside was a man's wedding ring, a wide band with oak leaves inlaid into its surface. "See if it fits," she said.

We now approach two decades married, and I sometimes still wonder at what love has wrought. I sometimes think Belinda might see in me a thing to nurture, a place to sacrifice, an altar on which to offer love. But I also feel something else—that glow from two decades ago, that heat between a woman and her mate.

Cynics say romantic love is a fiction. I have been thoroughly in love only once, and I think it a mystery, an enigma, a Gordian knot entwining two spirits. But even now I cannot fully resolve myself to the reality of Belinda's love. I chose to love Belinda, chose against my head-logic and with my heart-dreams. And even now, I confront the tasks with which she helps me each day with a mixture of guilt and gratitude, resentment and appreciation, anger and bemusement.

And somewhere deep in my psyche an old ugly beggar sleeps, unaware that the man Belinda chose to love has gotten on his horse and ridden away.

Gary Presley is the author of Seven Wheelchairs: A Life beyond Polio. *His essay appeared in November 2009.*

TRULY, MADLY, GUILTILY

AYELET WALDMAN

I HAVE BEEN IN MANY MOTHERS' GROUPS—MOMMY and Me, Gymboree, Second-Time Moms—and each time, within three minutes, the conversation invariably comes around to the topic of how often mommy feels compelled to put out. Everyone wants to be reassured that no one else is having sex, either. These are women who, for the most part, are comfortable with their bodies, consider themselves sexual beings. These are women who love their husbands or partners. Still, almost none of them is having any sex.

There are agreed-upon reasons for this bed death. They are exhausted. It still hurts. They are so physically available to their babies—nursing, carrying, stroking—how could they bear to be physically available to anyone else?

But the real reason for this lack of sex, or at least the most profound, is that the wife's passion has been refocused. Instead of concentrating her ardor on her husband, she concentrates it on her babies. Where once her husband was the center of her passionate universe, there is now a new sun in whose orbit she revolves. Libido, as she once knew it, is gone, and in its place is all-consuming maternal desire. There is absolute unanimity on this topic, and instant reassurance.

Except, that is, from me.

I am the only woman in Mommy and Me who seems to be, well, getting any. This could fill me with smug well-being. I could sit in the room and gloat over my wonderful marriage. I could think about how our sex life—always vital, even torrid—is more exciting and imaginative now than it was when we first met. I could check my watch to see if I have time to stop at Good Vibrations to see if they have any exciting new toys. I could even gaze pityingly at the other mothers in the group, wishing that they, too, could experience a love as deep as my own.

But I don't. I am far too busy worrying about what's wrong with me. Why, of all the women in the room, am I the only one who has not made the erotic transition a good mother is supposed to make? Why am I the only one incapable of placing her children at the center of her passionate universe?

When my first daughter was born, my husband held her in his hands and said, "My God, she's so beautiful."

I unwrapped the baby from her blankets. She was average size, with long, thin fingers and a random assortment of toes. Her eyes were close set, and she had her father's hooked nose. It looked better on him.

She looked like a newborn baby, red and scrawny, blotchy-faced and mewling. I don't remember what I said to my husband. Actually I remember very little of my Percocet- and Vicodin-fogged first few days of motherhood except for a friend calling and squealing, "Aren't you just completely in love?" And of course I was. Just not with my baby.

I do love her. But I'm not in love with her. Nor with her two brothers or sister. Yes, I have four children. Four children with whom I spend a good part of every day: bathing them, combing their hair, sitting with them while they do their homework, holding them while they weep their tragic tears. But I'm not in love with any of them. I am in love with my husband.

It is his face that inspires in me paroxysms of infatuated devotion. If a good mother is one who loves her child more than anyone else in the world, I am not a good mother. I am in fact a bad mother. I love my husband more than I love my children.

An example: I often engage in the parental pastime known as God Forbid. What if, God forbid, someone were to snatch one of my children? God forbid. I imagine what it would feel like to lose one or even all of them. I imagine myself consumed, destroyed by the pain. And yet, in these imaginings, there is always a future beyond the child's death. Because if I were to lose one of my children, God forbid, even if I lost all my children, God forbid, I would still have him, my husband.

But my imagination simply fails me when I try to picture a future beyond my husband's death. Of course I would have to live. I have four children, a mortgage, work to do. But I can imagine no joy without my husband.

I don't think the other mothers at Mommy and Me feel this way. I know they would be absolutely devastated if they found themselves widowed. But any one of them would sacrifice anything, including their husbands, for their children.

Can my bad motherhood be my husband's fault? Perhaps he just inspires more complete adoration than other husbands. He cooks, cleans, cares for the children at least 50 percent of the time.

If the most erotic form of foreplay to a mother of a small child is, as I've heard some women claim, loading the dishwasher or sweeping the floor, then he's a master of titillation.

He's handsome, brilliant, and successful. But he can also be scatterbrained, antisocial, and arrogant. He is a bad dancer, and he knows far too much about Klingon politics and the lyrics to Yes songs. All in all, he's not that much better than other men. The fault must be my own.

I am trying to remember those first days and weeks after giving birth. I know that my sexual longing for my husband took a while to return. I recall not wanting to make love. I did not even want to cuddle. At times I felt that if my husband's hand were to accidentally brush against my breast while reaching for the saltshaker, I would saw it off with the butter knife.

Even now I am not always in the mood. By the time the children go to bed, I am as drained as any mother who has spent her day working, carpooling, building Lego castles, and shopping for the precisely correct soccer cleat. I am also a compulsive reader. Put together fatigue and bookwormishness, and you could have a situation in which nobody ever gets any. Except that when I catch a glimpse of my husband from the corner of my eye—his smooth, round shoulders, his bright blue eyes through the magnification of his reading glasses—I fold over the page of my novel.

Sometimes I think I am alone in this obsession with my spouse. Sometimes I think my husband does not feel as I do. He loves the children the way a mother is supposed to. He has put them at the center of his world. But he is a man and thus possesses a strong libido. Having found something to usurp me as the sun of his universe does not mean he wants to make love to me any less.

And yet, he says I am wrong. He says he loves me as I love him. Every so often we escape from the children for a few days. We talk about our love, about how much we love each other's bodies and brains, about the things that make us happy in our marriage.

During the course of these meandering and exhilarating conversations, we touch each other, we start to make love, we stop.

And afterward my husband will say that we, he and I, are the core of what he cherishes, that the children are satellites, beloved but tangential. He seems entirely unperturbed by loving me like this. Loving me more than his children does not bother him. It does not make him feel like a bad father. He does not feel that loving me more than he loves them is a kind of infidelity.

And neither, I suppose, should I. I should not use that wretched phrase "bad mother." At the very least, I should allow that, if nothing else, I am good enough. I do know this: when I look around the room at the other mothers in the group, I know that I would not change places with any of them.

I wish some learned sociologist would publish a definitive study of marriages where the parents are desperately, ardently in love, where the parents love each other even more than they love the children. It would be wonderful if it could be established, once and for all, that the children of these marriages are more successful, happier, live longer, and have healthier lives than children whose mothers focus their desires and passions on them.

But even in the likely event that this study is not forthcoming, even in the event that I face a day of reckoning in which my children, God forbid, become heroin addicts or, God forbid, are unable to form decent attachments and wander from one miserable and unsatisfying relationship to another, or, God forbid, other things too awful even to imagine befall them, I cannot regret that when I look at my husband I still feel the same quickening of desire that I felt twelve years ago when I saw him for the first time, standing in the lobby of my apartment building, a bouquet of purple irises in his hands.

And if my children resent having been moons rather than the sun? If they berate me for not having loved them enough? If they call me a bad mother?

I will tell them that I wish for them a love like I have for their father. I will tell them that they are my children, and they deserve both to love and be loved like that. I will tell them to settle for nothing less than what they saw when they looked at me, looking at him.

Ayelet Waldman is the author of A Really Good Day *and other books. She lives in Berkeley with her husband and children. This essay appeared in March 2005.*

WHO'S THAT LADY IN THE BEDROOM, DADDY?

TREY ELLIS

I HEAR THEM BEFORE THEY COME IN, ALL THUMPS and frantic whispers in the hall outside my bedroom. Then the door opens just enough for their shoulders and elbows to jostle through as they compete to be first, followed by the melody of my own personal alarm clock: "Daddy, it's seven o'clock."

That's my daughter, who's six. She climbs onto the bed and presses her face next to mine.

I open one eye and see hers, huge. Then my son climbs onto the bed and across the landscape of the comforter, hammering my shins with his knobby little knees. "Daddy, it's seven o'clock," he parrots. He's three and a half.

And just like that, most every morning for the three years since my wife moved out, my big bed's emptiness is full again.

My bed is a vast California king made of Swedish memory foam developed by NASA. Both my son and daughter were conceived on this space-age polymer, and their first pushes from the womb took place here before the urgency of the situation hurried us to the hospital.

But only seven months after my son was born, I found myself alone on the springy expanse. My son was sleeping in his crib. My daughter was in her toddler bed. And my wife was in her bohemian studio on Venice Beach.

She wanted her freedom. I wanted stability for our kids. So she left, and I stayed, but I was a mess. Shocked and needy, I was desperate for solace.

Most of my male friends and all of my female ones cautioned me against rushing into another relationship, but I was convinced that what I most needed to help heal my heart was the smell of new skin. I threw myself into every singles bar in my area code, but always left as alone as I'd entered, and for months my personal real estate languished on the market.

Finally a veteran divorcé gave me this advice: "Think about all the women you wanted to sleep with when you were married, and call them."

A few days later I was driving home, top down, wind blowing the tears straight back to my ears, when I shouted to myself the name of a girl I'd always liked, a thirtysomething Nigerian who'd come by way of Liverpool.

When I got home I scavenged my oldest address books, found a number, dialed it, and amazingly, she answered. Sputtering, I told her my wife and I had divorced and I was calling to ask her out.

After a long silence she said, "I don't think so. You're still married."

True, the Dissolution of Marriage paperwork had been filed with the court only recently, and it would take another six months to be finalized. Luckily my soon-to-be ex-wife happened to be in the house at the time, watching the kids. We had always shared parenting duties, and our hours didn't change much after she moved out.

"Look, I'll put her on the phone, and you can ask her yourself."

I held my hand over the receiver and briefed my soon-to-be ex on the problem at hand. She took the phone into the other room.

What an odd life mine has become, I remember thinking.

Finally she returned and handed me the phone.

"Well, that's a first, Ellis," the Nigerian purred. "You must really want to go out with me."

Going out was one thing, but introducing new women to my kids was another. I was determined not to be one of those fathers who presented his kids with a new potential stepmother every few months. My ex and I even codified a waiting period into our Dissolution of Marriage agreement requiring us to wait six months before introducing to the children anyone we'd gotten serious about.

Since I'm the one still living with the kids, that deal is a whole lot easier for her than for me. It's a good plan, and it's been my fervent intention to abide by it. But navigating a new girlfriend into and out of my California king without my son or daughter noticing is sometimes a nerve-racking exercise in intrafamilial spycraft.

On my third date with the Nigerian, we'd gone back to my house after dinner. It was getting late, and hope was rising in me almost as quickly as terror. Would I break down and sob in the middle of it all? During those twelve years with the same woman had all my techniques become as clunky and unfashionable as Phil Collins and boxy suits?

But the next morning, I awoke alongside her in my bed both amazed and relieved—then terrified. My clock said 6:59. I jumped into my sweatpants, intercepted the kids on the stairs, and deftly steered them downstairs with a bribe: "French toast! Who wants French toast?"

I stuffed them with half a loaf and flooded each piece with syrup, hoping they'd pass out from the sugar buzz so I could sneak the Nigerian out of my house. Alternately, I was praying she would somehow take it upon herself to climb out the window and scale down the bougainvillea. Instead she flounced down the stairs and joined us in the breakfast nook—wearing my robe. My heart convulsed, but luckily the kids, who were only four years and eighteen months at the time, just giggled.

After that experience, during those agonizingly rare yet wonderful moments when a woman did find her way into my bed, I would have to explain to her up front that in my house checkout was sometime before dawn.

And then came the French woman. (I know—I go for international types. I can't help it.) She was twenty-seven. I was forty-one. Of course it was a cliché. Of course my friends threatened to schedule an intervention. And of course I didn't listen.

She and I had known each other for a year, e-mailing sporadically. Then one weekend, in Paris, we fell in love.

Two weeks later, I was meeting her at LAX with a rose, so nervous I could hardly stand.

I explained to my ex that our six-month rule couldn't possibly apply to overseas lovers, could it? Who could afford three weeks in a Los Angeles hotel? So Frenchie stayed with me and the kids, but we didn't kiss in front of them, determined to take it slow. Then, somehow, our jokes about marriage became more serious. Less than two months after that first weekend, we were engaged. Instead of being petrified or repulsed by the idea of becoming an instant mother, she said she craved it. She loved my kids, photographing them incessantly, teaching them to bake fondant au chocolat.

When my little boy claimed he was too tired to walk to the car, and I declined to carry him, it was she who hauled him up against her chest, where he clung like a contented monkey. She even said she wanted us to start trying for our own child in the fall. I'd thought I was done with diapers, and yet the idea of having a child with her made me smile.

We planned a midsummer civil ceremony, to be held at her parents' fairy-tale village in Bordeaux. We pictured our families settled around one of those impossibly long tables in the middle of a golden field, a band of old French drunkards crooning with accordions and such. Then in January she returned to Paris for a month and only sent an e-mail back. A long one.

I made the mistake of opening it in the middle of a typical morning of crazed parenting. My son was not quite out of diapers, and I found myself changing him on the washing machine while my heart battered my insides like an unbalanced load. I swallowed hard and explained to my kids that plans had changed and that Frenchie wasn't coming back. Ever. It's been over a year and a half, and sometimes my son still says he misses her.

Over the following months I finally came to peace with my fate, and I told myself I didn't need to look any further for love than the little ones I had helped create. I figured if I was kind to them and didn't damage them with scolding or indifference, their love for me wouldn't dissolve like the two great romances of my life. I decided that even if the rest of my life did proceed without a mate, I'd already been served a greedy helping of love.

And once I came to that conclusion, of course, I met a woman, Cris, an Italian who's not just lovely but closer to my age. It's now been five months, and she's flown in three times, and the kids haven't even seen us hold hands. During each of her visits she's stayed in a hotel down the street, and I've been setting the alarm for six to sneak her out. We want to be sure. We want to be surer than sure. But how can you ever be sure enough?

She arrives again in three weeks, our six-month anniversary, and we've decided it's time she be allowed to stay in my bed past the bewitching hour. We know each other well, though she can't yet really comprehend the entire package. She also has survived divorce but has no children of her own, so we'll see how she accepts my extremely cute and talkative baggage.

I was prepping the kids for this great shift when my son gave me a troubled look. "Will we still be able to cuddle in the morning?"

I cuddled him right then and said, "Of course, it's a California king. There's room for everyone."

And it's true: there is room for everyone in that big, comfy bed.

If only it were that simple.

Trey Ellis is a writer and professor living in Connecticut. This essay, which inspired his memoir, Bedtime Stories: Adventures in the Land of Single Fatherhood, *appeared in June 2005.*

YOU MAY WANT TO MARRY MY HUSBAND

AMY KROUSE ROSENTHAL

I HAVE BEEN TRYING TO WRITE THIS FOR A WHILE, but the morphine and lack of juicy cheeseburgers (what has it been now, five weeks without real food?) have drained my energy and interfered with whatever prose prowess remains. Additionally, the intermittent micronaps that keep whisking me away midsentence are clearly not propelling my work forward as quickly as I would like. But they are, admittedly, a bit of trippy fun.

Still, I have to stick with it, because I'm facing a deadline, in this case, a pressing one. I need to say this (and say it right) while I have (a) your attention and (b) a pulse.

I have been married to the most extraordinary man for twenty-six years. I was planning on at least another twenty-six together.

Want to hear a sick joke? A husband and wife walk into

the emergency room in the late evening on September 5, 2015. A few hours and tests later, the doctor clarifies that the unusual pain the wife is feeling on her right side isn't the no-biggie appendicitis they suspected but rather ovarian cancer.

As the couple head home in the early morning of September 6, somehow through the foggy shock of it all, they make the connection that today, the day they learned what had been festering, is also the day they would have officially kicked off their empty-nestering. The youngest of their three children had just left for college.

So many plans instantly went poof.

No trip with my husband and parents to South Africa. No reason, now, to apply for the Harvard Loeb Fellowship. No dream tour of Asia with my mother. No writers' residencies at those wonderful schools in India, Vancouver, Jakarta.

No wonder the words *cancer* and *cancel* look so similar.

This is when we entered what I came to think of as Plan "Be," existing only in the present. As for the future, allow me to introduce you to the gentleman of this article, Jason Brian Rosenthal.

He is an easy man to fall in love with. I did it in one day.

Let me explain: My father's best friend since summer camp, "Uncle" John, had known Jason and me separately our whole lives, but Jason and I had never met. I went to college out east and took my first job in California. When I moved back home to Chicago, John—who thought Jason and I were perfect for each other—set us up on a blind date.

It was 1989. We were only twenty-four. I had precisely zero expectations about this going anywhere. But when he knocked on the door of my little frame house, I thought, *Uh-oh, there is something highly likable about this person.*

By the end of dinner, I knew I wanted to marry him.

Jason? He knew a year later.

I have never been on Tinder, Bumble, or eHarmony, but I'm going to create a general profile for Jason right here, based on my experience of coexisting in the same house with him for, like, 9,490 days.

First, the basics: He is five-foot-ten, 160 pounds, with salt-and-pepper hair and hazel eyes.

The following list of attributes is in no particular order because everything feels important to me in some way.

He is a sharp dresser. Our young adult sons, Justin and Miles, often borrow his clothes. Those who know him—or just happen to glance down at the gap between his dress slacks and dress shoes—know that he has a flair for fabulous socks. He is fit and enjoys keeping in shape.

If our home could speak, it would add that Jason is uncannily handy. On the subject of food—man, can he cook. After a long day, there is no sweeter joy than seeing him walk in the door, plop a grocery bag down on the counter, and woo me with olives and some yummy cheese he has procured before he gets to work on the evening's meal.

Jason loves listening to live music; it's our favorite thing to do together. I should also add that our nineteen-year-old daughter, Paris, would rather go to a concert with him than anyone else.

When I was working on my first memoir, I kept circling

sections my editor wanted me to expand upon. She would say, "I'd like to see more of this character."

Of course, I would agree—he was indeed a captivating character. But it was funny because she could have just said: "Jason. Let's add more about Jason."

He is an absolutely wonderful father. Ask anyone. See that guy on the corner? Go ahead and ask him; he'll tell you. Jason is compassionate—and he can flip a pancake.

Jason paints. I love his artwork. I would call him an artist except for the law degree that keeps him at his downtown office most days from nine to five. Or at least it did before I got sick.

If you're looking for a dreamy, let's-go-for-it travel companion, Jason is your man. He also has an affinity for tiny things: taster spoons, little jars, a mini-sculpture of a couple sitting on a bench, which he presented to me as a reminder of how our family began.

Here is the kind of man Jason is: He showed up at our first pregnancy ultrasound with flowers. This is a man who, because he is always up early, surprises me every Sunday morning by making some kind of oddball smiley face out of items near the coffeepot: a spoon, a mug, a banana.

This is a man who emerges from the minimart or gas station and says, "Give me your palm." And, voilà, a colorful gumball appears. (He knows I love all the flavors but white.)

My guess is you know enough about him now. So let's swipe right.

Wait. Did I mention that he is incredibly handsome? I'm going to miss looking at that face of his.

If he sounds like a prince and our relationship seems like a fairy tale, it's not too far off, except for all of the regular stuff that comes from two and a half decades of playing house together. And the part about me getting cancer. Blech.

In my most recent memoir (written entirely before my diagnosis), I invited readers to send in suggestions for matching tattoos, the idea being that author and reader would be bonded by ink.

I was totally serious about this and encouraged submitters to be serious as well. Hundreds poured in. A few weeks after publication in August, I heard from a sixty-two-year-old librarian in Milwaukee named Paulette.

She suggested the word *more*. This was based on an essay in the book where I mention that *more* was my first spoken word (true). And now it may very well be my last (time shall tell).

In September, Paulette drove down to meet me at a Chicago tattoo parlor. She got hers (her very first) on her left wrist. I got mine on the underside of my left forearm, in my daughter's handwriting. This was my second tattoo; the first is a small, lowercase *j* that has been on my ankle for twenty-five years. You can probably guess what it stands for. Jason has one too, but with more letters: *AKR*.

I want more time with Jason. I want more time with my children. I want more time sipping martinis at the Green Mill Jazz Club on Thursday nights. But that is not going to happen. I probably have only a few days left being a person on this planet. So why I am doing this?

I am wrapping this up on Valentine's Day, and the most genuine, non-vase-oriented gift I can hope for is that the right person reads this, finds Jason, and another love story begins.

I'll leave this intentional empty space below as a way of giving you two the fresh start you deserve.

With all my love, Amy

A bestselling author of books for children and adults, Amy Krouse Rosenthal excelled at making many other things too, including short films and salads. She died of ovarian cancer on March 13, 2017, ten days after this essay was published.

HOLDING ON
THROUGH THE CURVES

A BODY SCARRED,
A MARRIAGE HEALED

AUTUMN STEPHENS

I GOT THE CALL ON A SUNNY JULY MORNING IN 2001, while my husband was at work and my children were in day care, and big, blowsy roses bloomed like crazy all over my backyard. According to the biopsy, the milk ducts of my right breast were riddled with cancer cells. Latent cells, at the moment, but if they ever took it into their pointy little heads to detonate, the oncologist said, all hell could break loose.

He suggested we go for the preemptive strike and fight it. And who was I to argue? One of my late-life babies was still in diapers, the other barely able to write his name. We would try a lumpectomy, we decided. If that didn't work, we would just cut the breast off.

My husband took the news of my illness stoically, almost as if it were something he already knew. Not so much as an arched eyebrow revealed surprise or dismay. Like many men, he prefers take-charge calm to histrionics. So, for that matter, do I. But that night, there was no sleep for me: I lay in the dark, trembling and alone with my fears. My husband could live without me, I knew. He had done so before—by choice. Despite his bouts of ambivalence about our marriage—and consequently, mine—I have been with (and without, and then with again) this man for more than a quarter of a century. Not all scars are visible to the naked eye.

Incomprehensible, it sometimes seems, that the Volvo-driving, tax-paying, insomniac mortgage holder whose ring I wear on my fourth finger was once a gangly nineteen-year-old who so stirred my soul, the blue-eyed boyfriend I met in the college co-op we both lived in, a haven for latter-day hippies and student activists. We became lovers one early spring night when the lights went out at a party fueled by alcohol and LSD. All winter, we had been circling each other: He was afraid, I realize now, of my sharp tongue; I suspected (not altogether incorrectly) that he was a much nicer person than I.

We had never been on a date, never engaged in any of the formal rituals of courtship that previous generations took for granted. But that night, in the dark, we found each other, and in the months and years that followed, while other couples merged and broke apart and merged again in new configurations, we stayed together. Eventually we married, then promptly betrayed each other in ways both explicit and ephemeral. For us there was to be no giddy, go-for-broke flush of newlywed euphoria; no honeymoon babies and no grand real estate purchase demonstrating our faith in a shared future. When the going got tough, there was nothing concrete to tie us down.

Two years to the date from our barefoot beachside wedding, my husband said he wanted a divorce. For weeks afterward, I felt so shattered that I was sometimes afraid to move, lest I fall apart; so susceptible to rejection that I scarcely dared show my wounded face, my loser's face, to the winner-loving world.

You can get used to anything, though. Here is what my new single life was like: lonely, liberating, productive. Quiet, in contrast to the silent, screaming despair that had characterized my marriage. And safe. Alone, I could not be stabbed in the back, my serenity hijacked by someone else's demons. Over time I settled deeply into myself. Sometimes, writing on deadline, I didn't leave my apartment for two or three days; I barely slept or changed my clothes. This I perceived not as pathology but pleasure, the full expression of a certain driven, antisocial aspect of myself that I tend to experience, or perhaps merely to romanticize, as the "real" me.

So when, five years later, my husband and I suddenly and unexpectedly reconciled (a chance meeting, an explosive kiss, déjà vu all over again) I thought hard before consenting to give up my bachelor-girl studio. With some misgiving, I co-signed the loan application for the big gray Victorian in Berkeley that we planned to fill, as soon as possible, with a family.

And then the aforementioned rose garden, and dinner parties, and the great relief of our parents that there would be grandchildren after all. Snapshot of a Happy Couple, at long last. Although a more penetrating portrait, a marital biopsy, would have revealed how mistrust still constricted the woman's heart; how the husband bloodied his inner cheek with his teeth, biting back his frustration. History repeats itself, doesn't it? For many years I waited, harboring my bitterness, for the other shoe to drop.

And so, finally, it did—although not quite in the fashion I had expected but with a diagnosis of cancer. The easy trade I thought I'd brokered—my saggy, forty-three-year-old breast in return for a shot at a nice, long, quotidian life—didn't go off as smoothly as I had anticipated. Neither my doctors nor my husband and I were shocked when the lesser surgical evil, lumpectomy, failed to rout the cancer. No one had promised it would. What came as a bolt from the blue was the raging postsurgical infection that blindsided me two days later and from which I did, in fact, almost die.

The summer of 2001 slipped away as I lay in bed, hooked up to IV meds, too preoccupied with my own condition to notice time passing. It took weeks of those IVs, first at the hospital, then at home, before I was healthy enough to have my breast—what remained of it, anyway—removed.

When the plastic surgeon talked about repairing my mutilated chest, reconstruction was the term he used. The word always makes me think of the Civil War: the blood-soaked battlefields, the doomed effort to heal and move on while the smell of death still hangs in the air.

I rejected his proposition out of hand. To be fair, there were medical reasons. But there were other reasons, too. Back when my husband and I were young, the feminist party line was that man-woman differences should not be emphasized. Perhaps because of that, I have seldom been able to summon—much less sustain—a viable sense of femi-

ninity. In fact, I've never even really understood what people mean by the word, but whatever it is, I am certain that a
matched set of mammaries doesn't define it.

And yet, as my appetite vanished and my weight dropped
to what it was in sixth grade, sometimes, thinking of how
fragile I looked and how wounded and delicate I felt, the
word *feminine* did indeed float into my mind. A bud on a
severed branch. Even now, noticing a newly patched portion of a city street, the dark asphalt scar, I am acutely aware
of my upper chest. That flat, empty surface where I sometimes feel tingling and sometimes feel pain, but where most
of the time I feel nothing.

But my husband: let's not forget about my husband. For
of course this is not my history alone. During that time, it
could not escape my captive attention how much my husband, my once ambivalent husband, cared for me. The man
cared—specifically and pragmatically. With his own two
hands, he bandaged the nothingness that I did not want to
see. Uncomplainingly drained the plastic tubing that drew
pus and blood from my chest; matter-of-factly measured
that foul fluid in a cup and recorded its quantity, as the surgeon had blithely, sadistically ordered us to do. And over
and over, the ritual of scrubbing skin, smoothing the latex
gloves over his familiar, competent hands, inserting the IV
into my tense but upturned arm, until finally my apprehen-
sion subsided and I looked up with unadulterated trust into
his tired but still-blue eyes.

There are easier ways to heal a marriage than by getting
cancer. But that is how it was for us. Do not, however, imagine us with our gazes forever entwined, our lips locked in a
grand finale kiss. Life goes on. And like many women in

their forties, I lament that my libido is not what it once was. I'm preoccupied with the children or work, or I'm simply weary, thinking of nothing except how much I would like to be asleep. The last thing I want to do is to move, or be moved. Nor do missing body parts tend to have an aphrodisiac effect on the flickering spark of midlife sex drive. I'm speaking strictly for myself here; my husband doesn't seem to mind. Make no mistake: if we were to divorce again, it would be from lack of sex, not lack of breasts.

But you're not thinking, are you, that I should be grateful that my husband still finds me alluring, that he cleaves to my disfigured side? I concede it's not the ideal denouement, to forsake all others for someone who turns out, in the end, to be so nakedly flawed. Yet haven't we all done precisely that, every one of us who has ever vowed fidelity to another imperfect human being?

Believe me, if I could, I'd spread myself out on the sheets like a lush landscape of sensual delights, the full complement, everything a lover could desire. But I do what I can; I make a sporadic effort, and it is true that we are close to each other afterward. He wraps his arm around my shoulder, and I attempt to amuse him, or at least to speak of topics other than our boys' behavior and tasks that remain to be done.

One afternoon last summer, my then three-year-old and I were strolling down the sidewalk, pausing, as we do, to examine the many objects of interest—pebbles, ants, cigarette butts. That day we were in luck: a gorgeous trumpet flower, orange and mauve and, indeed, somewhat resembling a miniature musical instrument, had fallen from the vine. But when my happy boy held up the blossom for me to admire, he saw that the underside was mottled and brown. Consternation wrestled with determination on his young face. "Mommy," he said, his voice quavering, "can we pretend it's perfect?"

In pretending, we sometimes forget. But in pretending, we also remember. Naked before the mirror, I marvel at the sight of my ribs, now so cleanly articulated. Mine—mine in part, anyway—is the bony, unembellished torso of a teenage boy, not unlike that of my husband at nineteen, when sex was the sticky glue that bonded us, blurring boundaries so that it was impossible to tell where one of our bodies stopped, where the other began. But now, of course, it's obvious which is mine. Mine is the one with the thin pink scar running northeast to southwest, pointing toward my heart.

Autumn Stephens is the editor of Roar Softly and Carry a Great Lipstick: 25 Women Writers on Life, Sex, and Survival *(Inner Ocean Publishing), from which this November 2004 essay was adapted.*

DJ'S HOMELESS MOMMY

DAN SAVAGE

THERE WAS NO GUARANTEE THAT DOING AN OPEN adoption would get us a baby any faster than doing a closed or foreign adoption. In fact, our agency warned us that, as a gay male couple, we might be in for a long wait. This point was driven home when both birth mothers who spoke at the two-day open adoption seminar we were required to attend said that finding "good, Christian homes" for their babies was their first concern. But we decided to go ahead and try to do an open adoption anyway. If we became parents, we wanted our child's biological parents to be a part of his life.

As it turns out, we didn't have to wait long. A few weeks after our paperwork was done, we got a call from the agency. A nineteen-year-old homeless street kid—homeless by choice and seven months pregnant by accident—had selected us from the agency's pool of prescreened parent wannabes.

The day we met her, the agency suggested that all three of us go out for lunch—well, four of us if you count Wish, her German shepherd; five if you count the baby she was carrying. We were bursting with touchy-feely questions, but she was wary, only interested in the facts: She didn't want to have an abortion and couldn't bring up her baby on the streets. That left adoption. And she was willing to jump through the agency's hoops—which included weekly counseling sessions and a few meetings with us—because she wanted to do an open adoption, too.

We were with her when DJ was born. And we were in her hospital room two days later when it was time for her to give him up. Before we could take DJ home, we literally had to take him from his mother's arms as she sat sobbing in her bed.

I was thirty-three years old when we adopted DJ, and I thought I knew what a broken heart looked like, how it felt, but I didn't know anything. You know what a broken heart looks like? Like a sobbing teenager handing over a two-day-old infant she can't take care of to a couple who she hopes can.

Ask a couple hoping to adopt what they want most in the world and they'll tell you there's only one thing on earth they want: a healthy baby. But many couples want something more: They want their child's biological parents to disappear permanently so there will never be any question about who their child's "real" parents are. The biological parents showing up on their doorstep, lawyers in tow, demanding their kid back is the collective nightmare of all adoptive parents, endlessly discussed in adoption chat rooms and during adoption seminars.

But it seemed to us that all adopted kids eventually want to know why they were adopted, and sooner or later they start asking questions. "Didn't they love me?" "Why did they throw me away?" In cases of closed adoptions there's not a lot the adoptive parents can say. Fact is, they don't know the answers. We would.

Like most homeless street kids, our son's birth mother works a national circuit. Portland or Seattle in the summer; Denver, Minneapolis, Chicago, and New York in the late summer and early fall; Phoenix, Las Vegas, or Los Angeles in the winter and spring. Then she hitchhikes or rides the rails back up to Portland, where she's from, and starts all over again. For the first few years after we adopted DJ, his mother made a point of coming up to Seattle during the summer so we could get together. When she wasn't in Seattle she kept in touch by phone. Her calls were usually short. She would ask how we were, we'd ask her the same, then we'd put DJ on the phone. She didn't gush; he didn't know what to say. But it was important to DJ that his mother called.

When DJ was three, his mother stopped calling regularly and stopped visiting. When she did call, it was usually with disturbing news. One time her boyfriend had died of alcohol poisoning. They were sleeping on a sidewalk in New Orleans, and when she woke up, he was dead. Another time she called after her next boyfriend started using heroin again. Soon the calls stopped, and we began to worry about whether she was alive or dead. After six months with no contact, I started calling hospitals. Then morgues.

When DJ's fourth birthday came and went without a call, I was convinced that something had happened to her on the road or in a train yard somewhere. She had to be dead.

I was tearing down the wallpaper in an extra bedroom one night shortly after DJ turned four. His best friend, a little boy named Haven, had spent the night, and after Haven's mother picked him up, DJ dragged a chair into the room and watched as I pulled wallpaper down in strips.

"Haven has a mommy," he suddenly said, "and I have a mommy."

"That's right," I responded.

He went on. "I came out of my mommy's tummy. I play with my mommy in the park." Then he looked at me and asked, "When will I see my mommy again?"

"This summer," I said, hoping it wasn't a lie. It was April, and we hadn't heard from DJ's mother since September of the previous year. "We'll see her in the park, just like last summer."

We didn't see her in the summer. Or in the fall or spring. I wasn't sure what to tell DJ. We knew that she hadn't thrown him away and that she loved him. We also knew, though, that she wasn't calling and could be dead. In fact, I was convinced she was dead. But dead or alive, we weren't sure how to handle the issue with DJ. Which two-by-four to hit him with? That his mother was in all likelihood dead? Or that she was out there somewhere but didn't care enough to come by or call? And soon he would be asking more complicated questions. What if he wanted to know why his mother didn't love him enough to take care of herself? So she could live long enough to be there for him? So she could tell him herself how much she loved him when he was old enough to remember her and to know what love means?

My partner and I discussed these issues late at night, when DJ was in bed, thankful for each day that passed without the issue of his missing mother coming up. We knew we wouldn't be able to avoid or finesse the issue after summer arrived in Seattle. As the weeks ticked away, we admitted to each other that those closed adoptions we'd frowned upon were starting to look pretty good. Instead of being a mystery, his mother was a mass of very distressing specifics. And instead of dealing with his birth parent's specifics at, say, eighteen or twenty-one, like many adopted children, he would have to deal with them at four or five.

He was already beginning to deal with them: The last time his mother visited, when DJ was three, he wanted to know why she smelled so terrible. We were taken aback and answered without thinking it through. We explained that, since she doesn't have a home, she isn't able to bathe often or wash her clothes.

We realized we'd screwed up even before DJ started to freak. What, after all, could be more terrifying to a child than the idea of not having a home? Telling him that his mother chooses to live on the streets, that for her the streets were home, didn't cut it. For months DJ insisted that his mother was just going to have to come and live with us. We had a bathroom, a washing machine. She could sleep in the guest bedroom. When Grandma came to visit, she could sleep in his bed and he would sleep on the floor.

We did hear from DJ's mother again, fourteen months later, when she called from Portland, Oregon. She wasn't dead, only thoughtless. She'd lost track of time and didn't make it up to Seattle before it got too cold and wet; and whenever she thought about calling it was either too late or she was too drunk. When she told me she'd reached the point where she got sick when she didn't drink, I gently suggested that maybe it was time to get off the streets, stop drinking and using drugs, and think about her future. I could hear her rolling her eyes.

The reason she'd chosen us over all the straight couples was because we didn't look old enough to be her parents. She didn't want us to start acting like her parents now, she said. She would get off the streets when she was ready. She wasn't angry and didn't raise her voice. She just wanted to make sure we understood one another.

DJ was happy to hear from his mother, and the fourteen months without a call or a visit were forgotten. We went down to Portland to see her, she apologized to DJ in person, we took some pictures, and she promised not to disappear again.

We didn't hear from her for a year. This time she wasn't drunk. She was in prison, charged with assault. She'd been in prison before, for short stretches, picked up on vagrancy and trespassing charges. But this time was different—she needed our help. Or her dog did.

Her boyfriends and traveling companions were always vanishing, but her dog, Wish, was the one constant presence in her life. Having a large dog complicates hitchhiking and hopping trains, of course, but DJ's mother is a petite woman, and her dog offers her some protection. And love.

Late one night in New Orleans, she told us from a noisy common room in the jail, she'd gotten into an argument with another homeless person. He lunged at her, and Wish bit him. She was calling, she said, because it didn't look she would get out of prison before the pound put Wish down.

She was distraught. We had to help her save Wish, she begged. She was crying, the first time I'd heard her cry since that day in the hospital six years before.

Five weeks and $1,600 later, we had managed not only to save Wish but also to get DJ's mother out and the charges dropped. When we talked on the phone, I urged her to move on to someplace else. I found out three months later that she'd taken my advice—she was calling from a jail in Virginia, where she'd been arrested for trespassing at a train yard. Wish was okay—he was with friends; she was only calling to say hello to DJ.

I've heard people say that choosing to live on the streets is a kind of slow-motion suicide. Having known DJ's mother for six years now I'd say that's accurate. Everything she does seems to court danger. I've lost track of the number of her friends and boyfriends who have died of an overdose, alcohol poisoning, or hypothermia.

As he gets older, DJ is getting a more accurate picture of his mother, but so far it doesn't seem to be an issue for him. He loves her. A photo of a family reunion we attended isn't complete, he insists, because his mother isn't in it. He wants to see her this summer, "even if she smells," he says. We're looking forward to seeing her, too. But I'm tired.

Now for the may-God-rip-off-my-fingers-before-I-type-this part of the essay: I'm starting to get anxious for this slo-mo suicide to end, whatever that end looks like. I'd prefer that it end with DJ's mother off the streets, in an apartment somewhere, pulling her life together. But as she gets older that resolution is getting harder to picture.

A lot of people who self-destruct don't think twice about destroying their children in the process. Maybe DJ's mother knew she was going to self-destruct and loved DJ so much that she wanted to make sure he wouldn't get hurt. She left him somewhere safe, with parents she chose for him, even though it broke her heart to give him away, because she knew that if he were close she would hurt him, too. Sometimes I wonder if this answer will be good enough for DJ when he asks us why his mother couldn't hold it together just enough to stay in the world for him. I kind of doubt it.

Dan Savage is the author of The Commitment: Love, Sex, Marriage, and My Family, *from which this September 2005 essay was adapted.*

NOW I NEED A PLACE TO HIDE AWAY

ANN HOOD

IT IS DIFFICULT TO HIDE FROM THE BEATLES. AFTER all these years they are still regularly in the news. Their songs play on oldies stations, countdowns, and best-ofs. There is always some Beatles anniversary: the first Number One song, the first time in the United States, a birthday, an anniversary, a milestone, a Broadway show.

But hide from the Beatles I must. Or, in some cases, escape. One day in the grocery store, when "Eight Days a Week" came on, I had to leave my cartful of food and run out. Stepping into an elevator that's blasting a peppy Muzak version of "Hey Jude" is enough to send me home to bed.

Of course it wasn't always this way. I used to love everything about the Beatles. As a child I memorized their birthdays, their tragic life stories, the words to all of their songs. I collected Beatles trading cards in bubble gum packs and

wore a charm bracelet of dangling Beatles' heads and guitars.

For days my cousin Debbie and I argued over whether
"Penny Lane" and its flip side, "Strawberry Fields Forever,"
had been worth waiting for. I struggled to understand *Sgt.
Pepper.* I marveled over the brilliance of the *White Album.*

My cousins and I used to play Beatles wives. We all
wanted to be married to Paul, but John was okay, too. None
of us wanted Ringo. Or even worse, George.

It was too easy to love Paul. Those bedroom eyes. That
mop of hair. Classically cute. When I was eight, I asked
my mother if she thought I might someday marry Paul
McCartney.

"Well, honey," she said, taking a long drag on her Pall
Mall. "Somebody will. Maybe it'll be you."

In fifth grade, in a diary in which I mostly wrote, *It is so
boring here,* or simply, *Bored,* only one entry stands out: *I
just heard on the radio that Paul got married. Oh, please, God,
don't let it be true.*

It was true, and I mourned for far too long.

Of course by the time I was in high school, I understood
my folly. John was the best Beatle: sarcastic, funny, interesting looking. That long thin nose. Those round wire-
rimmed glasses. By then I didn't want to be anybody's wife.
But I did want a boy like John, someone who spoke his
mind, got into trouble, swore a lot, and wrote poetry.

When I did get married and then had children, it was
Beatles songs I sang to them at night. As one of the youngest
of twenty-four cousins, I had never held an infant or baby-
sat. I didn't know any lullabies, so I sang Sam and Grace to

sleep with "I Will" and "P.S. I Love You." Eventually Sam fell in love with Broadway musicals and abandoned the Beatles.

But not Grace. She embraced them with all the fervor that I had. Her taste was quirky, mature.

"What's the song where the man is standing, holding his head?" she asked, frowning, and before long I had unearthed my old *Help!* album, and the two of us were singing, "Here I stand, head in hand."

For Grace's fourth Christmas, Santa brought her all of the Beatles' movies on video, a photo book of their career, and the *1* tape. Before long, playing "Eight Days a Week" as loud as possible became our anthem. Even Sam sang along and admitted that it was arguably the best song ever written.

Best of all about my daughter the Beatles fan was that by the time she was five, she already had fallen for John. Paul's traditional good looks did not win her over. Instead she liked John's nasally voice, his dark side. After watching the biopic *Backbeat,* she said Stu was her favorite. But soon she returned to John. Once I overheard her arguing with a first-grade boy who didn't believe that there had been another Beatle.

"There were two other Beatles," Grace told him, disgusted. "Stu and Pete Best." She rolled her eyes and stomped off in her glittery shoes.

Sometimes, before she fell asleep, she would make me tell her stories about John's mother dying, how the band met in Liverpool, and how when Paul wrote the tune for "Yesterday," he sang the words "scrambled eggs" to it.

After I would drop Sam off at school and continue with

Grace to her kindergarten, she'd have me play one of her Beatles tapes. She would sing along the whole way there: "Scrambled eggs, all my troubles seemed so far away."

On the day George Harrison died, Grace acted as if she had lost a friend, walking sad and teary-eyed around the house, shaking her head in disbelief. She asked if we could play just Beatles music all day, and we did. That night we watched a retrospective on George. Feeling guilty, I confessed that he was the one none of us wanted to marry.

"George?" Grace said, stunned. "But he's great."

Five months later, on a beautiful April morning, Grace and I took Sam to school, then got in the car and sang along with "I Want to Hold Your Hand" while we drove. Before she left, she asked me to cue the tape so that as soon as she got back in the car that afternoon, she could hear "You've Got to Hide Your Love Away" right from the beginning. That was the last time we listened to our Beatles together.

The next day Grace spiked a fever and died from a virulent form of strep. Briefly, as she lay in the ICU, the nurses told us to bring in some of her favorite music. My husband ran out to his car and grabbed *1* from the tape deck. Then he put it in the hospital's tape deck, and we climbed on the bed with our daughter and sang her "Love Me Do." Despite the tubes and machines struggling to keep her alive, Grace smiled at us as we sang to her.

At her memorial service, eight-year-old Sam, wearing a bright red bow tie, stood in front of the hundreds of people there and sang "Eight Days a Week" loud enough for his sister, wherever she had gone, to hear him.

That evening I gathered all of my Beatles music—the dusty albums, the tapes that littered the floor of my car, the CDs that filled our stereo—and put them in a box with Grace's copies of the Beatles movies. I could not pause over any of them.

Instead I threw them in carelessly and fast, knowing that the sight of those black-and-white faces on *Revolver,* or the dizzying colors of *Sgt. Pepper,* or even the cartoon drawings from *Yellow Submarine,* the very things that had made me so happy a week earlier, were now too painful even to glimpse. As parents do, I had shared my passions with my children. And when it came to the Beatles, Grace had seized my passion and made it her own. But with her death, that passion was turned upside down, and rather than bring joy, the Beatles haunted me.

I couldn't bear to hear even the opening chords of "Yesterday" or a cover of "Michelle." In the car I started listening only to talk radio to avoid a Beatles song catching me by surprise and touching off another round of sobbing.

I tried to shield myself from the Beatles altogether—their music, images, conversations about them—but it's hard, if not impossible. How, for example, am I supposed to ask Sam not to pick out their music slowly during his guitar lessons?

Back in the sixties, in my aunt's family room, with the knotty-pine walls and Zenith TV, with my female cousins all around me, our hair straight and long, our bangs in our eyes, the air thick with our parents' cigarette smoke and the harmonies of the Beatles, I believed there was no love greater than mine for Paul McCartney.

Sometimes now, alone, I find myself singing softly. "And when at last I find you, your song will fill the air," I sing to Grace, imagining her blue eyes shining behind her own little wire-rimmed glasses, her feet tapping in time. "Love you whenever we're together, love you when we're apart." It was once my favorite love song, silent now in its *White Album* cover in my basement.

How foolish I was to have fallen so easily for Paul while overlooking John and George, to have believed that everything I could ever want was right there in that family room of my childhood: cousins, TV, my favorite music. But mostly I feel foolish for believing that my time with my daughter would never end.

Or perhaps that is love: a leap of faith, a belief in the impossible, the ability to believe that a little girl in a small town in Rhode Island would grow up to marry Paul McCartney. Or for a grieving woman to believe that a mother's love is so strong that the child she lost can still hear her singing a lullaby.

Ann Hood lives in Providence, Rhode Island. Her most recent book is Kitchen Yarns: Notes on Life, Love, and Food. *This essay appeared in February 2006.*

JUST HOLDING ON THROUGH THE CURVES

CRIS BEAM

MY DAUGHTER JUST TURNED THIRTY. HOW IS this possible when it seemed like only a week before she was a scrappy, sassy teenager? Like mothers everywhere, I don't think I'm old enough to have delivered a baby girl who could hit such a milestone.

In my case, it's true: I'm only forty-one. I didn't give birth to my daughter. I became her mother when I was twenty-eight and she was seventeen. Call it an unplanned delivery, very late term. Christina was one of the 135,000-plus teenagers nationwide in foster care, most of whom are abandoned when they age out of the system between eighteen and twenty-one.

I was lucky enough to snare one of these gems, to share my life with the smartest, most beautiful, resourceful, and hilarious kid around.

Want proof? I have pictures. But be careful what you ask for: like mothers everywhere, I'm insufferable that way.

I say I'm lucky because I didn't plan for this life. Back when everything happened, Christina was just my favorite student in the high school English class I was teaching. When her agency made her change schools, we stayed in touch.

There was something both fierce and vulnerable about Christina, and I liked being with her. She is also deeply intelligent, and I wanted to ensure that no matter how the world tossed her around, at least one of her teachers had shown her that she mattered.

I also wanted to keep an eye on her safety. Christina is transgender, which meant there were fewer beds available to her within the system and fewer protections over all.

Sure enough, at her new school, disaster struck: After a security guard told some of her fellow students she had been born male, they threatened to kill her, so she fled. I was the first person she called, and my then-partner and I offered to let her sleep on our couch until we could sort things out with the agency. Anyone with a conscience would have done the same.

What I didn't understand at the time was how profoundly child welfare can fail its teenagers. I didn't know that fully half of all the teenagers in foster care are institutionalized in group homes or more serious lockdown facilities because families don't want them.

I didn't know that, by age nineteen, 30 percent of the boys will have been incarcerated. I didn't know, as Christina's first night bled into a second and a third and as we went to Home Depot to buy containers for her clothes and cleared her a shelf in the bathroom, that 30 percent of the homeless in this country were once in foster care.

Most of us can't survive our first jobs, first apartments, first loves, or first big mistakes without family to fall back on. We need money, love, advice, and encouragement well past our eighteenth birthdays—especially if we celebrated that birthday in an institution with state-financed guardians working eight-hour shifts.

What I did know, as I tucked sheets into Christina's makeshift bed those first few nights, was that I had a hurt and angry child on my hands who was frightened of being rejected one more time. And I knew that child because I had been one, too.

When I was fourteen, I left my mother's house and never saw her again. I moved to my father's house thirty miles away. My mother didn't reach out or call, and I was too afraid to reach back to the woman who didn't want me.

When I graduated from college, I sent my mother a letter, and she sent me a note on a paper scrap, wishing me a good life and misspelling my name. Later I recognized the signs of mental illness in her; I recognized it in the men she brought around, in the nights she didn't come home, in the way she'd drift into corners and lose herself all day.

But I didn't know to call it that when I was a child. Mostly I scuttled about like a dog on ice trying to make her better. Mostly I thought my mother's rejection was my fault. And when I couldn't take it anymore, I left.

When Christina moved in, I wasn't blind to the symmetry. I saw how in helping her I could repair some of my own story; I could be the mother that my mother never was. But just as Christina was settling into a kind of routine in our little one-bedroom apartment, her agency called to say she couldn't stay.

We already had enrolled her in a new public school and were working on her résumé so she could get a job. We were redistributing household chores. But we weren't licensed foster parents, so they had found her space in a group home for teenage sex offenders.

Christina had never committed such a crime and was understandably terrified. It would be only for a while, they promised, until they could find something better.

The thing is, I was the "something better." I had already been found, and Christina was safe with me. I wasn't going to let a broken system break down a child I loved. I hadn't planned on being a mother to a teenager at twenty-eight, but I discovered if you threaten an injured cub in my den, I could become a mother right quick.

Together we fought back, and after some heated phone calls and hasty arrangements, she ended up with us. But that isn't the triumphal part of the story. The triumph is the past thirteen years.

Being a parent to a teenager can be like driving a racecar on a slick track with no brakes. The radio blares Spanish rap and the kid in the passenger seat hurls catcalls at passing drivers and then ducks, or threatens to hurl herself out the door if she's angry with you. Oh, wait—maybe that's just my teenager.

Anyway, I learned that with my teenager you just have to hold on through the curves. I didn't learn to be a great mother the way I had planned, but I did learn that no "bad" behavior by her would ever warrant the ultimate rejection.

I learned there's not one child worth discarding—not the tens of thousands of children in group homes, not Christina, not even me.

That last part was Christina's gift. The bonus was realizing that the teenage thing passes. And then you get the glorious young adult who suddenly, miraculously, loves you back.

My experience of Christina's childhood was extraordinarily compressed. I didn't get the diapers or teething or first haircuts. But I did get her first steps. There was the time she started meeting her curfew because she "didn't want to worry" me, even though she had never kept a curfew before. (Nobody had cared before.)

My ex and I used to wake her up with Dolly Parton's song "Little Sparrow," which she claimed to hate, because it was the only thing that got her out of bed. When she turned nineteen, she got a sparrow tattoo as a tribute.

And finally there was the letter, a few years back, in which she thanked me for saving her life. She had saved her own life, I told her, but it takes depth of soul to feel such gratitude.

Besides, I'm the one who's grateful. I wish more people would want to foster teenagers (although they, like me, may not consider it until one lands in their lap). Unlike the littler children, teenagers often recognize that their frustrations and sorrows are born of the system and their families of origin, rather than you.

They can say, as Christina often did when she was in a rage: "I don't know why I'm even acting this way. It's probably from the abuse in one of my homes."

And I could say: "I don't know what to do with you. I have no experience."

And we both could then shrug at our respective confusion and order a pizza to eat together on the couch.

The triumph in the story isn't that we celebrated Christina's eighteenth and nineteenth and twenty-fifth birthdays and that she never even came close to becoming one of those sad foster-care statistics. The triumph is that we celebrated them together. And Christina's family has grown: She has made inroads with her biological relatives and kept my ex as her other mother; last summer Christina was a part of her wedding.

My current partner and I recently traveled to see Christina for her birthday and to mark the moment over Korean barbecue the way we always do. Our messy family looks like a lot of messy families, but at the core, we stay close because we choose to. Christina taught me that a lasting family isn't something that happens, it's something you choose year after year.

Which means we actually like spending birthdays together. Even if thirty does sound awfully old.

It's OK. I'm still a very young mother.

Cris Beam is an author and professor in New York City. Her latest book is I Feel You: The Surprising Power of Extreme Empathy. *This essay appeared in August 2013.*

RALLYING TO KEEP
THE GAME ALIVE

ANN LEARY

WHEN I TOOK UP TENNIS, MY HUSBAND WAS
happy to play with our two children and me, as long
as we didn't have to play by the rules. As Denis repeatedly
explained to us, playing by the rules placed him at an unfair
disadvantage because he didn't know the rules, and he didn't
know how to serve.

Instead of learning the rules, he wanted to play a varia-
tion of tennis he had invented with another actor while on
location in a tropical country. Their game involved no serving and a complicated but curiously malleable set of rules
that often appeared, to me, to change midgame and almost
always to Denis's advantage.

This caused some heated courtside squabbles. I'm
ashamed to admit that one year we spent several days of
a family vacation not speaking to each other after a game
of "Denis Tennis" that I had lost "unfairly" (I repeatedly

hissed at our children), until finally our son and daughter had to intervene and coerce a truce between us.

This was a tricky time in our marriage. Though we had found tennis late, we had found each other quite early in our adult lives, and now we were going through a rough patch, one that had lasted for years.

When we met, I was twenty, he twenty-five. We were too young and inexperienced to know that people don't change who they are, only how they play and work with others. Our basic problem was, and is, that we are almost identical—in looks, attitudes, and psychological makeup. Two Leos who love children and animals and are intensely emotional and highly sensitive and competitive with everybody, but especially with each other.

When the children came along, we got caught up in the tallying of efforts, the scorekeeping of who was doing more for the marriage and family and who was being self-serving, unloving, and disapproving. We didn't bicker often, but when we fought, we raged.

Eventually we began to see a marriage counselor, who, among other things, suggested that we have a regular date night. Our apathy was such that our date night was our marriage-counseling night. Afterward we sometimes went to a movie. One of the movies we saw was *March of the Penguins*.

This movie moved us to tears because whatever battles raged between us, however ugly the other often appeared to be, we had these two very delicate fledglings that needed to be protected and carried along carefully, so carefully, because is anything more fragile than a preteenage girl or a growing, unsure boy?

These great children were the reason we were in counseling, the reason we were trying to keep the family egg whole. So we worked hard at playing nice. We had regular family nights and took family vacations. And on occasion we tried to play tennis together.

Despite all of this, the marriage continued to flounder, and the time came when we met in our marriage counselor's office and I said, "I think it's over."

"That's it," Denis agreed.

When we left, it felt as if we were floating, we were so calm. We had stormed out of those doors and stomped down those steps in such rages before, but now Denis held the door for me, and I thanked him. When we got to the street, it was snowing. I had boots with heels, and the sidewalks were icy. I couldn't walk on the icy sidewalks with those heels, so I asked if I could hold his arm, if he could walk me home.

"Sure," he said. He didn't care.

Neither did I. I just needed something to hold on to so I wouldn't slip and fall. I clung to his arm, and we bent our bodies into the wind.

"The thing is," he said as we walked, "I'm tired and hungry."

"Let's get something to eat," I said.

We went to the restaurant across from our building, a little neighborhood place where the waiters know our names and the chef knows how we like our burgers. We sat in a booth in the back. Denis ordered soup.

It was all over, there was nothing to lose, so I decided to serve up my final grievances, the things I felt he needed to know to fully understand that he was the cause of our marriage's untimely end. I reminded him, in a resigned tone, of the time he did this, the time he did that.

These were the wretched rags of resentment so bitter and old, so petty, that I had been too ashamed even to mention them in therapy, so now I balled them up and tossed them onto Denis's court.

Denis just ate his soup. When he was finished, he wiped his chin with his napkin. We were both so calm it was as if the island of Manhattan had been gassed with some kind of Valium vapor.

I guess there was no emotion left, it was all over, and we both experienced this finality as a surprising relief. We were like the penguin couple in *March of the Penguins* that accidentally dropped and broke their egg. They looked at the egg for a time, and then they parted ways, because penguins don't mate for life. They court each other, commit each other's voice to memory, produce an egg, devote themselves to its care, and when it dies, or matures, the parents part company.

This was how we had come to view our marriage, as a penguin marriage, a partnership devoted to raising children. We had hoped to stick it out until they left the nest, but now it looked as if that would be impossible. So we were just having a last look.

Denis carefully refolded his napkin, and then said: "I'm sorry. If I could change those things I would, but I can't. They're in the past. But, I'm sorry."

I had expected him to cry foul, to react the way he did when I said a questionable tennis shot of his was out. But he just said he was sorry. And I believed him. He had no reason to make up that kind of thing now.

His calm admission inspired me to exhale my own litany of regrets and apologies. In the movies, this would have been the moment we leapt into each other's embrace, but in real life, we ordered more food. We called the children in the apartment to see if they wanted to go to a movie. That night Denis didn't stay in a hotel; he stayed home. The next day we all drove to the country. The family, after all that mad jostling, somehow had remained intact.

So things got better. We went to our counselor. We went to our movies. We worked at treating each other more fairly. And we started playing a lot of tennis, just the two of us, whenever we could. Only now we played by the rules.

Though I had many lessons under my belt, Denis is the better athlete, so almost immediately we played on more or less the same level. We improved every game. We stopped cheating. (Yes, I admit, we both used to call questionable shots out when we were backed into a corner, and we used to fudge the score if we could, both of us.)

Though we were still ultracompetitive, we were becoming intensely proud when the other hit an amazing shot, and we didn't hate the winner when we lost. We still played to win, but now we could feel joy for the other. We wanted to improve, and now we wanted, were actually thrilled, to see the other get better, too.

Which brings me to our last game of that summer, the last before we packed up our son and drove him to college. We had each won a set, and now it was 5–5 in the final set. We had reserved the court for only an hour, though, and the hour was almost up. There were other players waiting. So this would have to be the final, and deciding, game of the match. But the games had been so hard-won that neither of us could bear to lose the match.

Denis was serving in this deciding game. He served carefully, not trying to ace it past me for once. It was too risky. I didn't take advantage by slamming my return into his backhand court. What if it went out? The match would be over.

I hit the ball into his court, and he hit it back into mine. I placed the ball in his court carefully, so carefully, and he placed it back in mine. We rallied, not with the adrenaline-pumping determination to win at all costs, but with the patience and control that came with not wanting it to be over: not the summer, not our son's childhood, not this game, ever.

Back and forth we sent the ball. And it occurred to me there was some sort of grace in my husband's form, and I felt it in mine, too, as we both worked to keep the game alive just a little longer, by trying to find each other's sweet spot, by playing, for once, to the other's advantage.

Ann Leary, a New York Times *bestselling author, lives in New York; her next novel will be published in 2020 by Simon & Schuster. This essay appeared in September 2013.*

OUT FROM UNDER THE INFLUENCE

KEVIN CAHILLANE

MY FIRST DATE WITH JULIE DID NOT BEGIN WELL and ended even worse. For starters, I didn't show. It was Saturday evening of Presidents' Day weekend, and I was drinking gin and tonics and watching hoops in the Telephone Bar and Grill on Second Avenue, whiling away the time before I was supposed to meet her at John's Pizzeria, just down the block. The next thing I knew it was hours later and the phone was waking me from my slumber in my apartment on East Twelfth Street.

I stumbled out of the building and ran to John's, where Julie ended up crying defiantly on the sidewalk, her words lost to me but their meaning clear: never again.

After she left in a cab for the Upper West Side, it could have been just one of those first dates from hell that eventually becomes funny in the retelling. But it wasn't that simple. We worked together at an advertising agency, she as a human resources coordinator and I as one of the human resources she coordinated. She was the first person I'd met at work. I'd only passed the typing test because she had added an extra five minutes to the egg timer.

With that and a smile she'd hooked me, and I started spending my nights constructing elaborate and clever e-mail messages to her that I would pass off as spontaneous the next day. She began to drop by my desk with a frequency that I attributed more to her need for my ragged charm than my need for the memos she was distributing.

Now all that groundwork appeared lost. And on Tuesday I'd have to face her again.

I continued to drink all weekend, wallowing in regret, and on Sunday I sent her a hundred dollars' worth of roses, bought with money I didn't have, along with a note of apology. Unfortunately I also left her a voice mail message that consisted of Hootie and the Blowfish's "Hold My Hand" in its entirety.

When Tuesday rolled around, I stayed home. Wednesday, the same.

I knew this kind of denial was not a practical long-term strategy, so on Thursday I got dressed and tried to return to work. But my nerves were shattered, my head cloudy. I had crossed the line, as I sometimes did, from functional alcoholic to clearly not.

Finally I called Julie. "Did you get the roses?" I asked.

Yes, she had, and they were lovely, but she felt it was a rather grotesque gesture all the same. "You're an alcoholic," she said, not unkindly. "You need help."

I had already reached this conclusion myself at age sixteen, but no one had ever said it directly to me. Julie suggested I make an appointment for the next morning with a doctor associated with the agency's employee-assistance program. I did. I was love-struck and free-falling, and if she'd asked me to jump off a bridge, I might have done that, too. But again I stumbled out of bed disoriented and arrived at the doctor's half an hour late, rain-soaked.

His West Fifty-seventh Street office was lush and quiet; somewhere a fountain trickled tranquilly. He was bearded and kindly but he got right to the point.

"Now, what brings you here?" he asked.

"I drink."

"How often?"

"Daily."

"Have you been drinking this morning?"

"Affirmative."

"What about your arm?"

"I have a cat."

"Must be some cat."

"I don't really have a cat."

"I think you like to see the physical manifestation of your psychic pain."

"Who doesn't?"

He diagnosed me with acute alcoholism, which wasn't exactly breaking news, and recommended that I seek treatment pronto at an inpatient rehabilitation clinic.

"If it's okay with Blue Cross," I told him, "it's okay with me."

I was twenty-four years old.

I returned to my apartment, where I hadn't paid rent in some time, and waited for a call from the benefits people at work. I had been with the agency for only six months, and only as a favor to my aunt, who had worked there for several years. From my shaggy wardrobe to my computer illiteracy, it was pretty clear I was not Madison Avenue material, but she had snagged me an interview anyway.

Julie, my unlikely advocate, called and told me that my benefits were shipshape and that I was good to go. So I went, but not before draining several forties to steel myself for the phone calls I had to make to family and friends to ensure that I wasn't reported AWOL.

When the van arrived to pick me up, the grizzled driver told me that most people were drunker than I was. Somehow this made me feel worse, as if I couldn't even self-destruct correctly. As the van sailed north on the FDR Drive, I thought the bright lights of the big city never looked quite so intoxicating as when you were leaving.

Nearly three weeks later I appeared at Julie's cubicle in my only suit. She hugged me and told me I looked great. I told her she did, too. She found some envelopes for me to stuff and papers to photocopy, tasks I completed with un-precedented zeal. She looked amused each time I reported on my progress and requested more work.

At the end of the day I took off my jacket, sat in her cu-bicle, and told her about rehab.

"Nobody thought you'd come back," she said.

As I got up to go, I briefly touched her knee as if I were some repressed character in a Merchant-Ivory movie, and then I walked home through the streets of Manhattan.

We met that weekend in Central Park and talked as we walked. Julie was from Canton, Ohio, a daughter of a school-teacher and a football coach. She was a Phi Beta something or other, and her best friend was her sister, a graphic designer in Chicago. She had chosen the ad agency over Merrill Lynch because it felt more humane. Me, I was just a guy from New Jersey whose path of least resistance had led through the Lincoln Tunnel.

The recovery literature warned of the dangers of starting a romance days (or even weeks, sometimes years) after coming out of the drink, but I wanted company on my lifeboat, and Julie seemed ready to grab an oar, if warily.

At our next date in the park, she climbed a rock and declared me too raw to date. "I think we should just be friends," she said.

I didn't begrudge her this decision. If you were to take Julie's suitors from over the years and place them in a police lineup, I clearly was the one who most likely belonged. We walked through the Ramble, across the Sheep Meadow, and to a clearing where the skyscraping hotels of Central Park South looked luminous in the gloaming. As the light disappeared behind the Palisades and a full moon shone, she turned to me and said, "If we weren't just friends, this would be kind of romantic."

During our hermetically sealed days and nights that followed, I made her a promise that I would stay sober.

Two months later, though, I was back with old friends and to my old self. Julie and I attended a wedding at the Jersey Shore, where, unbeknownst to her, I knocked back drink after drink. I simply could not see anything past the clinking ice cubes and undulating limes in seemingly every person's glass. I danced with the groom's sister, who whispered in my ear to give her a call if I ever decided to "lose the blonde." One old acquaintance looked at me quizzically as I poured a few back during our conversation and said, "You a little thirsty?"

On the return to the city, we became ensnarled in traffic awaiting a DWI checkpoint. Terrified, I kept up the ruse by telling Julie it was a good thing I'd quit drinking when I had. Such is the bottomless cup of duplicity that we drunks drink from. When the officer simply waved me through, I felt such joy and relief that I vowed I'd had my last drink. And except for a few minor lapses in the next month or so, it was.

Two years later, we were married on a steamy June day in a tiny church in an industrial corner of Canton as guests fanned themselves with their programs. The night before the wedding, a group of the hopeful and faithless had gathered for the rehearsal dinner in a restaurant in old downtown Canton. There was the requisite mix of drinks and well wishes, and I still had the sense that my mouth and arm could conspire against my brain to raise a little hell, but they didn't.

When it came my turn to toast, I recited the speech I had outlined on a cocktail napkin at the Indians game the night before. I forget every word of it now except for the last line, which I borrowed from a Bruce Springsteen song. I promised Julie that for better or worse, for richer or more likely poorer, I would love her with all the madness in my soul. It was one part vow, one part pose, and one part roll of the dice.

Then I lifted my glass in the air and put it back down.

It's been ten years since my last drink, and it's not like rolling a boulder up a mountain every day. In fact it's no effort at all. I don't attend meetings, speak in jargon, or mouth the Serenity Prayer when flummoxed. The accumulation of thousands of days without alcohol has simply made it a reflexive nonhabit.

Julie and I have ordinary jobs, a home in the suburbs, and a minivan for our 2.5 children (two now and one due in December), who, genetically speaking, could have hoped for better. Soon enough they will surely tell me so.

But I don't know. The thing is, would their mother and I ever have gotten together if I hadn't been a drowning alcoholic in need of her outstretched hand? Sometimes I can't help but wonder if the burdens we carry don't end up carrying us.

Kevin Cahillane is a copywriter and journalist who lives in Summit, New Jersey. This essay appeared in July 2005.

THE CHICKEN'S IN THE OVEN, MY HUSBAND'S OUT THE DOOR

THEO PAULINE NESTOR

SOME MARRIAGES GRIND SLOWLY TO A HALT. Others, like mine, explode midflight, a space shuttle torn asunder in the clear blue sky as the stunned crowd watches in disbelief. And the hazardous debris from the catastrophe just keeps raining down.

It was late September, still warm but past the last hot stretch of Indian summer. I had waited for a day cool enough to roast a chicken for my husband and two young daughters. When I put the five-pound chicken in the oven, a shower of fresh green herbs clinging to its breast, our marriage was still intact. By the time I pulled it out, my husband had left our house and driven away for good, his car stuffed with clothes slipping off their hangers.

It was my call to the bank to check our balance that caused the fatal blowup. Although my husband's destructive compulsions with money had threatened our marriage before, I believed those days were long behind us. But that afternoon, without even trying to, I discovered the truth: far from changing his ways, he had simply become more secretive. I confronted him. And that, as they say, was that.

So the roast chicken fed only one person that night: our nine-year-old daughter, Elizabeth. I couldn't eat, and our five-year-old, Grace, announced she wouldn't eat a real chicken, only chicken nuggets. I took the red box from the freezer, plucked out five tawny squares, heated them in the microwave, and placed them in front of Grace, who believed, as did her sister, that their father had gone downtown to meet a friend and that he and this friend were going on an impromptu car trip. "Dad will come home in a week," I told them. I didn't know what else to say.

I thought of my childhood friend Nancy, whose marriage had fallen apart a year earlier. I have three friends from childhood I am still close to; coincidentally, all four of us married around our thirtieth birthdays. For ten years we beat the odds. Then Nancy's marriage broke up, and now, with mine, our little group reflected that often-cited statistic: half of all marriages end in divorce.

At Nancy's wedding, the minister had briefly turned his attention from the newlyweds to address the group directly. "It is up to the community to hold a couple together," he had said in his commanding voice. "Each of you here is responsible for remembering for this couple the love that brought them together and the commitment they've made."

I took his words to heart, silently vowing to support Nancy and Terry, to remind Nancy of Terry's strengths someday when she might vent to me after a marital spat. Despite their vows and my support, despite ten years and two sons, their marriage couldn't be held together. And now, despite eleven years and two daughters, neither could mine.

The women I grew up with, like most women today, have tangible, marketable skills. One is an electrician, another a graphic artist, a third a nurse. Inside or outside a marriage, they can support themselves. I, too, am a well-educated woman with a decent work history, who actually made more money than my husband when we married. I prided myself on being self-sufficient. But we both wanted someone to be home with the kids, and we decided it would be me, so I stopped working and let him support us. And now I've ended up in the same vulnerable position I once thought was the fate only of women who married straight out of high school, with no job experience beyond summer gigs at the Dairy Queen.

Not that I would have done it differently. I have valued my time with our daughters more than any other experience I've had. But for a stay-at-home mom like me, divorce isn't just divorce. It's more like divorce plus being fired from a job, because you can no longer afford to keep your job at home, the one you gave up your career for. When I worked as an English professor at the community college, we called people like me displaced homemakers. I imagined legions of gingham-aproned Betty Crockers spinning perpetually, forever tracing their feather dusters across imaginary furniture, never ceasing to "make" the "home" that was no longer there. Now that my income has dwindled to child support and a meager "maintenance" check, I must leave this job and get a "real" one. I add up our expenses for a month and then subtract his contribution. The remaining total indicates that to keep the girls and myself out of debt, I will need to net a third more than the most I've ever made.

And divorce is its own job, with its course of study, its manuals. One of the many divorce books heaped on the floor beside my bed urges me to develop two stories about the breakup: a private one and a public one. I'm told that I should practice a few sentences that I can recite (in the grocery store, on the playground) without excessive emotion, a sort of campaign slogan for my divorce. And it does seem as if much of my daily work involves negotiating the snowy pass between my private and public self. Alone, I shriek into my pillow, and I shout "Bonehead!" through the closed car window as I drive past my ex's new apartment. In public, I am stoic, detached, nodding philosophically as a married mother from Elizabeth's soccer team tells me, "Your grief is like a house. One day you'll be in the room of sorrow and the next you might be in anger."

A humbled divorcée, I can only act as if all this is news to me.

"And oh, denial!" she adds. "That's a room, too—don't forget."

Eventually you have to tell everyone who hasn't heard through the grapevine. Some people get "the whole story" and some just get the abridged "we've separated" version.

The whole-story people are exhausting. At first it's all relief and adrenaline as you recount the moment you realized the shuttle was breaking apart. But then you are overwhelmed with dread as you come to understand how many whole-story people there are in your life. Still ahead are countless oh-my-gods and I'm-so-sorrys and you-must-be-kiddings. You hear sympathetic and understandable questions coming at you, and your tongue grows thick and unfamiliar forming all those words one more time. You consider a form letter:

Dear Good Friend Who Deserves the Whole Story,

I'm sorry this is coming to you as a form letter.
I'm sorry about a lot.
I'm just sorry.

Or perhaps there could be a website: www.whatthehell happened.com, complete with a FAQ link.

Q. *What about the children?*
A. *They live with me but will stay with him every Friday and every first, third, and fifth Thursday night as well as the first Saturday of every month. Yes, it's hard to remember which week it is.*
Q. *Will reconciliation be possible?*
A. *No. If you read the whole story you will understand why. (Use password to access the secure site.)*
Q. *Are you okay?*
A. *No, I'm not. Thanks for asking.*
Q. *Is there anything we can do to help?*
A. *Yes. Click on the Send Money link below.*

When I took off my wedding rings, my finger had atrophied underneath in a manner that seems excessively symbolic. I protect this white band with my thumb like a wound. I look at other women's ring fingers: gold bands, simple solitaires, swirling clusters of diamonds. The fact that they've managed to keep those rings in place seems miraculous, a defiance of gravity. When I wore my rings, I was a different person, emboldened in the way one can be in a Halloween costume. I could laugh as loudly as I wanted and go out with dirty hair and in sweatpants. I was married. Someone loved me, and it showed. I could refer to a husband in conversations with a new friend or a store clerk. They didn't care if I was married or not, but I did. My ring said, You can't touch me. It's like base in a game of tag. You're safe.

Now when I go to bed I turn the electric blanket to high and let the heat soak into my skin. Sometimes, lying here, I think of this divorce business as something like the flu. The feverish beginnings, as miserable and sweaty as they are, are somehow easier to get through (they are a blur, really) than the many half-well, half-sick days that follow, days when you're not sure what to do. You're too well to lie in bed watching TV but too sick to go out and do all the things well people are expected to do.

To fall asleep, I resort to the old routine of counting my blessings. I count my daughters over and over again. I count their health, their happiness, the gift of who they are.

I urge myself to find something else I am grateful for but can't. And then I realize there is something.

It's this rawness of spirit, the way the crust of my middle-age shell has been blown off me, and here I am, the real me. I am no longer the person who can pretend everything's okay. I can no longer think of myself as "safe" or protected. I know now it is up to me to hunt, to gather, and to keep shelter warm.

Theo Pauline Nestor lives in Kitsap County in Washington State. Her most recent book is Writing Is My Drink: A Writer's Story of Finding Her Voice (and a Guide to How You Can Too). *This essay appeared in November 2004.*

TAKE ME AS I AM, WHOEVER I AM

TERRI CHENEY

A S A BIPOLAR WOMAN, I HAVE LIVED MUCH OF my life in a constant state of becoming someone else. The precise term for my disorder is *ultraradian rapid cycler*, which means that without medication I am at the mercy of my own spectacular mood swings: "up" for days (charming, talkative, effusive, funny, and productive, but never sleeping and ultimately hard to be around), then "down," and essentially immobile, for weeks at a time.

This darkness started for me in high school, when I simply couldn't get out of bed one morning. No problem, except I stayed there for twenty-one days. As this pattern continued, my parents, friends, and teachers grew concerned, but they just thought I was eccentric. After all, I remained a stellar student, never misbehaved, and graduated as class valedictorian.

Vassar was the same, where I thrived academically despite my mental illness. I then sailed through law school and quickly found career success as an entertainment lawyer in Los Angeles, where I represented celebrities and major motion picture studios. All the while I searched for help through an endless parade of doctors, therapists, drugs, and harrowing treatments like electroshock, to no avail.

Other than doctors, nobody knew. At work, where my skills and productivity were all that mattered, I could hide my secret with relative ease. I kept friends and family unaware with elaborate excuses, only showing up when I was sure to impress.

But my personal life was another story. In love there's no hiding: You have to let someone know who you are, but I didn't have a clue who I was from one moment to the next. When dating me, you might go to bed with Madame Bovary and wake up with Hester Prynne. Worst of all, my manic, charming self was constantly putting me into situations that my down self couldn't handle.

For example: One morning I met a man in the supermarket produce aisle. I hadn't slept for three days, but you wouldn't have known it to look at me. My eyes glowed green, my strawberry blond hair put the strawberries to shame, and I literally sparkled (I'd worn a gold sequined shirt to the supermarket—manic taste is always bad). I was hungry, but not for produce. I was hungry for him, in his well-worn jeans, Yankees cap slightly askew.

I pulled my cart alongside his and started lasciviously squeezing a peach. "I like them nice and firm, don't you?"

He nodded. "And no bruises."

That's all I needed, an opening, and I was off. I told him

my name, asked him his likes and dislikes in fruit, sports, presidential candidates, and women. I talked so quickly I barely had time to hear his answers.

I didn't buy any peaches, but I left with a dinner date on Saturday, two nights away, leaving plenty of time to rest, shave my legs, and pick out the perfect outfit.

But by the time I got home, the darkness had already descended. I didn't feel like plowing through my closet or unpacking the groceries. I just left them on the counter to rot or not rot—what did it matter? I didn't even change my sequined shirt. I tumbled into bed as I was, and stayed there. My body felt as if I had been dipped in slow-drying concrete. It was all I could do to draw a breath in and push it back out, over and over. I would have cried from the sheer monotony of it, but tears were too much effort.

On Saturday afternoon the phone rang. I was still in bed, and had to force myself to roll over, pick it up, and mutter hello.

"It's Jeff, from the peaches. Just calling to confirm your address."

Jeff? Peaches? I vaguely remembered talking to someone who fit that description, but it seemed a lifetime ago. And that wasn't me doing the talking then, or at least not this me—I'd never wear sequins in the morning. But my conscience knew better. "Get up, get dressed!" it hissed in my ear. "It doesn't matter if she made the date, you've got to see it through."

When Jeff showed up at seven, I was dressed and ready, but more for a funeral than a date. I was swathed in black and hadn't put on any makeup, so my naturally fair skin looked ghostly and wan. But I opened the door, and even held up my cheek to be kissed. I took no pleasure in the feel of his lips on my skin. Pleasure was for the living.

I had nothing to say, not then or at dinner. So Jeff talked, a lot at first, then less and less until finally, during dessert, he asked, "You don't by any chance have a twin, do you?"

And yet I was crushed when he didn't call.

A couple of weeks later, I awoke to a world gone Disney: daffodil sunshine, robin's-egg sky. Birds were trilling outside my window, a song no doubt created especially for me. I couldn't stand it a minute longer. I flung back the covers and danced in my nightie—my gray flannel prison-issue nightie. I caught one glimpse of it in the mirror, shuddered, and flung it off, too.

I rifled through my closet for something decent to wear, but everything I put my hands on was wrong, wrong, wrong. For starters, it was all black. I hated black, even more than I hated gray. Redheads should be true to their colors, whatever the cost. I dug deeper, and there, shoved way in the back, was a pair of skintight jeans and something silky and sparkly and just what I needed: an exquisite gold sequined shirt.

I slipped it on and preened for a minute. Damn, I looked good. Then I tugged on the jeans. I had gained a few pounds during the last couple weeks of slothlike existence, but once I yanked really hard, they zipped up fine. Although something was sticking out of the pocket: a business card, with a few words scribbled across the back: *Call me, Jeff.*

Jeff?

Jeff! I kicked the nightie out of my way and grabbed the bedside phone. Was 6:30 a.m. too early to call? No, not for good old Jeff! It rang and rang. I was about to give up when a thick, sleepy voice said "Hello?"

"It's me! Why haven't you called?"

It took a while to establish who "me" was, but eventually he remembered. "You sound different," he said. "Or no, maybe you sound more like yourself. I'm not sure. It's so early."

Soon I had him laughing so hard he got the hiccups and had to get off the phone. But before he did, he asked me out for Friday, three nights away.

No, I insisted, it had to be tonight, or even this afternoon. I didn't want to lose another chance to get to know him. I knew that Cinderella had only so much time left at the ball.

We compromised on dinner that evening at eight. I spent the afternoon ridding my house of all evidence of depression. I soaped and scoured and dusted and vacuumed, using every attachment, even the ones that frightened me. Then I ran out and bought a dozen Casablanca lilies to hide the smell of ammonia and bleach.

When the house looked perfect, I turned on myself with the same fury. I buffed and polished and creamed and plucked and did everything in my power to re-create Rita Hayworth's smoky allure in *Gilda*. As I was shadowing my eyes, I remembered her poignant line about the movie: "Every man I've known has fallen in love with Gilda, and wakened with me." It gnawed at me, to the point that my hand started trembling and I couldn't finish applying my mascara.

Suddenly I didn't look radiant. There were lines around my mouth and a hollowness to my eyes that aged me ten years. My skin, despite the carefully applied foundation and blush, was so deathly pale I recoiled from my reflection.

I sat on the toilet and started to cry. I had met the enemy enough times to know it by sight. *Not now,* I prayed. *Please not now.* Globs of mascara ran down my cheeks, and I wiped them away, heedless of the streaks they left. It was 7:57. I had three minutes to wrestle my brain chemistry into submission. Oh, sure, I knew there was another option. I could tell Jeff what was going on. But this was a man who didn't even like his peaches bruised. What would he think of a damaged psyche?

Maybe he would understand. Maybe I would find the courage. Maybe they would invent a cure.

Maybe, but not tonight. As the doorbell rang and rang, I huddled in the bathroom, shivering. I was terrified—not just of Jeff finding me there, but of me never once finding love.

When it was finally quiet, I rinsed off the rest of my mascara and tossed my cocktail dress into the hamper. Then I buttoned up my gray flannel nightie and settled in for the long night to come.

I never heard from Jeff again.

That was five years ago—five long years of ups and downs, of searching for just the right doctor and just the right dose. I've finally accepted that there is no cure for the chemical imbalance in my brain, any more than there is a cure for love. But there's a little yellow pill I'm very fond of, and a pale blue one, and some pretty pink capsules, and a handful of other colors that have turned my life around. Under their influence, I'm a different person yet again, neither Madame Bovary nor Hester Prynne, but someone in between. I have moods, but they don't send me spinning into an alternate persona.

Stability, ironically, is so exciting I have decided to venture into dating again. I have succumbed to pressure from friends and signed up for three months of a computer dating service. "Who are you?" the questionnaire asks at the start.

I want to be honest, but I don't know how to answer. Who am I now? Or who was I then?

Life seems so much tamer these days: deceptively quiet, like a tiger with velveted paws. Every so often the sun shines too bright and I think, for a moment, that I own the sky. I think, how wonderful it was to be Gilda, if only in my own mind. But then I remember the price of the sky. So I take off my makeup, rumple my hair, and go to the supermarket in sweats. The gold sequined shirt languishes in my closet. I'm thinking of giving it away.

Not just yet.

Terri Cheney is the author of the New York Times *bestseller* Manic, *and her stories and commentary are featured in her widely read* Psychology Today *blog and in her forthcoming book,* Tell Me Where It Hurts. *This essay appeared in January 2008.*

ADOLESCENCE, WITHOUT A ROADMAP

CLAIRE SCOVELL LaZEBNIK

A T LEAST HE'S GOOD-LOOKING," I SAY TO MY husband whenever the subject of our oldest son's dating future comes up. And he is good-looking, our son, with his blue eyes, wavy hair, broad shoulders, and warm smile. He's also got a deep voice (he works at it) and a gentle manner. It's hard to believe girls won't fall in love with him. And maybe they will.

But he also has autism. When he's tired or sick, he forgets words or uses them incorrectly; often it requires enormous effort just for him to maintain a conversation. It's as if he has no native tongue and essentially has had to memorize our language word by word.

Now he's working on our customs. You see him eagerly watching other kids, looking for clues and lessons, signs he can follow into the world of the average teenager. It's a world he's desperate to be part of. He dresses like them, adopts their gestures, mimics their rudeness, and even douses himself, as they do, with Axe deodorant body spray.

He'll be in the middle of a group of kids and they'll laugh. Then he'll laugh, a second too late and too loud. He knows he needs to laugh to fit in; that much he's learned from observation. What he can't seem to learn is what made the joke funny and why everyone gets it but him.

For a long time our son was a little boy with autism, which was a certain kind of challenge. Now that he's a teenager with autism—and a teenager who notices girls—we're faced with something else altogether.

"Hey, Mom?" he says as we're walking out of a store. "That girl was hot." He thinks he's talking in a whisper but he isn't, really, because he has voice modulation problems and has trouble hearing what his own voice sounds like. The lifeguard in the bikini at the beach is also "hot." So is Jessica Alba, whose picture he printed and carefully glued onto his binder, next to a photo of Keira Knightley.

The term *hot* may be an affectation he picked up from his friends, but his appreciation of skinny girls with big breasts seems to be genuine, as we realized when we discovered he'd started using the Internet the way other teenage boys are likely to only when they think no one is watching.

We put content filters on our browser software, and his father sat down with him to go over some basic rules: Wait until you're in love to have sex. Always wear a condom. Hide your pornography where your mother won't find it. He'll remember all this because they're rules, and he's very good at remembering rules.

It's the other stuff—the emotional, heart-stopping stuff—that's going to be hard.

I know he wants to find a girl and fall in love. Sometimes people say that kids with autism aren't capable of love. That's ridiculous. My son loves deeply. He just doesn't communicate well. The instincts we rely on when we're first falling in love (being able to sense what someone else is thinking, becoming aware of a sudden connection, anticipating another person's desire) don't come naturally to him.

I want the girls he meets to know that just because he speaks a little oddly and sometimes struggles to understand what they're saying doesn't mean he wouldn't make a great boyfriend. I want them to see what a good heart he has, how he would never manipulate or hurt them, how he would be grateful, obliging, and loyal. But how many girls will be able to get past the frustrations of his disabilities to appreciate that part of him?

Would I have been able to?

And these things can't be forced anyway, no matter how good-hearted someone may be.

Last year he got friendly with a girl he met in a social skills class. She was what those of us in the world of special needs describe as "lower-functioning." She attended a special-needs school, but even there she felt she was the object of ridicule and abuse. I never knew if her account of insults and cruelties was accurate, but I'd hear my son talking to her on the phone, offering his unwavering support. "That's terrible!" he'd cry out after listening for a while. "They shouldn't do that."

I'd listen to him and think, "What woman wouldn't want a man who comforted her like that, who was willing to listen and believe and always be on her side?" It gave me hope.

In the end, though, he broke up with her, if "breaking up" is even the right term for ending what they had. Her litany of complaints bored him. And in all honesty she wasn't the slightest bit "hot." Although he never mentioned it, I suspect this also may have been a factor in his decision.

Since then, the only girls he's asked out have been at the other end of the spectrum, and they've all rejected him—for the most part (and as far as I know)—quite kindly.

Still, he aims high. Recently he asked out a girl who was already dating the star athlete of the entire middle school, an eighth-grader who was captain of the baseball and basketball teams. When I suggested that maybe a girl like her was out of his reach, my son just looked confused. The social intricacies of popularity that separate students into cliques and loners mean nothing to him because they're unstated, unquantified. Most of us just sense them instinctively. He can't.

Obviously I could let myself be crushed by these rejections, especially if he were. But so far he doesn't seem to mind; there's an advantage to his emotional obliviousness. He's still young, though, and none of his friends is really dating, so he probably doesn't feel so left out yet. Still, I worry about whether girls will keep rejecting him throughout high school and into college, while the other kids start successfully pairing off. What if he starts to wonder if anyone will ever love him?

You can, I've discovered, teach your child to make polite conversation (ask questions, listen attentively, then ask more questions), to be a good host (offer refreshments, suggest activities, and choose the one your guest says he'll enjoy), to please his teachers (show up on time, behave well in class). But how do you teach him to fall in love with some-one who will love him back? What rules can you lay down for making someone's heart leap when she sees him?

When our son's autism was diagnosed at the age of two and a half, there was no clear prognosis. We didn't even know if he'd ever learn to talk. But we found talented people to work with him, and he improved, slowly at first and then more rapidly. By the time he graduated from elementary school, he had no discernible behavioral or academic prob-lems.

People congratulated us. Our son had emerged. Some-one met our kids at a party and a friend mentioned that one of them had autism. "Which one?" the person said, genu-inely bewildered, and then guessed the wrong child.

But that was from a distance. Up close it's clearer that our son is marked and challenged, fundamentally and per-manently. And up close is where relationships live. Up close is what love is all about. And sex? Well, that goes without saying.

This leads to what is perhaps the scarier question: What happens when a girl finally says yes? A year or two ago, going out meant nothing more than a kind of glorified play-date. But I overhear the kids in his class flirting, and there's a strong edge of sexuality to it. My son's body has matured, and physically, if not developmentally, he's not a little boy anymore.

Just as he's learned our language and our customs with a lot of hard work and memorization, he'll soon have to learn how to navigate the world of sex. But how? Through imitation and observation? Through rules we teach him? No. The same kids he has studied and imitated to gain other social skills are going to be fumbling in the dark themselves, behind closed doors. And in this particular game I don't foresee his father and me doing much coaching from the sidelines. He'll truly have to find his own way.

Then again, I've seen him rise to similar challenges in ways I never anticipated. I was told, for example, that kids with autism can't be empathetic because they're incapable of being able to perceive and relate to someone else's suffering. He can learn that he's supposed to say, "That's terrible!" when someone complains to him about an injustice. But the ability to notice and respond to the nuances of another person's emotions and moods isn't supposed to be in his repertory. And it's true that when he was younger I could sob in front of him (something I did all too often back then, I'm afraid), and he would simply continue his play, oblivious to my emotions.

Not long ago, however, when I was fixing a snack in the kitchen for all my kids while they sat around the table doing their homework, something about the situation reminded me of my mother, who'd died recently, and I quietly began to cry.

My three younger children didn't notice. But my son looked up and said, "What's wrong, Mom? Are you okay?" and came over to give me a hug. I literally smiled through my tears.

Somehow he had learned something they said couldn't be taught. I'll take that as a good sign.

Claire Scovell LaZebnik lives in Los Angeles and is the author of Things I Should Have Known. *This essay appeared in October 2005.*

MY HUSBAND IS NOW MY WIFE

DIANE DANIEL

THE ALARM SOUNDED AT 4 A.M. ON A TUESDAY last November. My husband and I had been told to arrive two hours early, as if for a flight. My eyelids were puffy from the night before, when he had held me and said he was sorry, so very sorry.

I'd wept without warning after dinner because I would not see his face again, his perfectly average face with a sizable nose and weak chin, the face I'd held and kissed and been happy to greet for eight years.

"Do you still have your wedding ring on?" I asked. "They said to take it off."

We'd married in our forties, both for the first time, our independent lives blending seamlessly.

"Oops, yes." He twisted the ring off his slender finger, and I placed it in a beaded box on my dresser. We'd bought the box on Bali, one of our many adventures. On that trip we shared crazy-hot meals, hiked up volcanic mountains, and stayed in a grungy room that housed a large lizard, a fact my considerate mate did not reveal until we checked out. My protector, my pal, my prince.

Here we were again, exploring new territory, headed to a place where we knew a few customs and words but were not fluent.

As he backed out of the driveway, I thought of the checklist and asked, "You didn't drink water, did you?"

"What do you mean?"

"The pre-op instructions. How much did you drink?"

"About half a cup," he confessed.

"Unbelievable," I huffed.

We rode in silence, anger masking my fear. I focused on my breathing, on letting my affection return like a ripple moving toward the shore.

"What are you feeling, hon?" I put a hand on his leg, returned to the person I usually am with him.

"Stupid for not reading the directions."

"Better than feeling afraid."

We were told the operation could last seven hours and recovery several more, so I came prepared, as on a trip, packing my laptop, phone, magazines, a blanket, and a pillow.

He checked in, and a nurse led us to a room where she checked his vitals, all excellent. His water transgression was deemed acceptable.

"He" checked in. "His" transgression.

Still, on this day, when my husband would take his first surgical step into womanhood, I continued to say "him," "his," and "he," even though our therapist had suggested for months that I use female pronouns at home.

"I will when I need to," I'd told her on our last visit. "But for now he's still a man to me." I'd turned to my husband, dressed in jeans and a black button-down shirt. "When I look at you, hon, I see a man."

"But she's a woman," our therapist countered, her words slicing through my denial.

"Not to me," I said with wet eyes. I crossed my arms like a willful child. "I can accept that he'll become a woman, but he's still a man now. How do you feel, hon? Do you really feel like you're a woman now?"

"I've told you before, yes, I feel like a woman," he said with an apologetic look.

And so the time when I "need to" had arrived. We were at the hospital for facial feminization surgery, a not uncommon procedure in male-to-female transitions, in which a surgeon carves out a more femininely proportioned version of a male face. In my husband's case, this meant higher eyebrows, a smaller nose, and a more pronounced chin. A few months later, his Adam's apple would be shaved down and he would receive breast implants. Genital surgery would follow.

Already, estrogen had narrowed and softened his face, and the alterations would be slight, the surgeon said. His wide blue eyes would not change, nor would his high-enough cheekbones or soft lips.

Our history of openness, affection, and trust had kept me believing that our relationship would survive, even thrive. I never felt my husband had deceived me, as some friends suggested. He had told me early on that he was am-bivalent about his maleness but had made peace with it. Having conflicted feelings about men myself, the macho sort, I hadn't realized the depth of his confusion.

It wasn't until we were married that my husband, finally feeling loved, admitted to himself that he was transgender. That he was, inside, a woman. That he did not want to be the man I married.

Stunned and wounded, I located a therapist, read transgender books, found support online, and confided in the lone friend I entrusted with my secret. My husband and I continued to talk, to love.

Over time I came to believe that my husband, as my wife, would be in most ways the same person: intelligent, compassionate, mature, with the same slim build. I'd had a relationship with a woman in my early twenties, so living as a lesbian was agreeable enough, though I mourned the societal ease we would lose.

In the pre-op room, I pulled my chair toward my husband's gurney. He was sitting up, shoulders stooped, feet hanging over the side. I buried my head in his chest.

The curtain moved and his surgeon appeared. "Good morning," she said cheerily. Seeing her outside her office jarred me. Surgery was no longer a plan, but an event. I started to cry—softly, politely—though I wanted to wail and sob. How do you grieve for someone you've lost but who is still there?

She took a surgical marker from her pocket and sat opposite my husband to draw black dots on his chin, nose, and forehead. When she was finished, he looked like a warrior.

She left us alone, and I took his hand in mine, my eyes now dry while his filled with tears.

"What's going on, hon?" I asked.

"I'm sorry for all the pain I'm causing you."

Tears smudged the dots under his nose and rolled down his face.

"I know why I'm doing all this, but it's just crazy, isn't it?" he said. "And I regret all the years I felt so isolated. I wonder what I missed."

"Try to focus on the courage you're showing by doing this at all."

The nurse returned. "It's time to go. Your husband will be fine," she added with a smile.

The outpatient waiting room was crowded with people anxious to hear about their families, friends, lovers. As I do on airplanes, I took a window seat. I saw that the day had dawned gray and rainy, with gusts of wind.

I overheard conversations about heart attacks, cancer, hip replacements, but nothing about gender transitions. Starting today, I would be a minority, an oddity: the wife of a transgender woman. The notion exhausted me.

I passed the hours reading and emailing updates to the small circle of family and friends who knew about the operation. Our official "coming out" email would be sent the following week.

The surgeon, all smiles, stopped by to let me know everything had gone smoothly. A few hours later, a nurse took me to my wife, to her—those terms I must start saying. Her bruised face was compressed with bandages while another strip of gauze was taped under her nose. She was groggy and hurting.

"After he eats a little something, we'll give him pain pills," a nurse said.

"Could you say 'she'?" I asked gently.

Two hours later, as the sun set, we headed home. I'd reclined her seat, propped my pillow under her head, and laid my blanket over her. I drove carefully, placing my hand on her knee whenever I could.

When we reached the house, I asked if she minded staying in the car while I tended to the pets, knowing our entrance would be chaotic otherwise. She nodded yes.

The house was warm, but I turned the heat up to make it toasty. I imagined my life if the person in the car didn't exist. Easier, but empty.

I returned and roused my dozing partner, spouse, wife. We shuffled inside and into our bedroom, which I'd stocked with her medications, ice bags, and gauze. I maneuvered her under the covers and fluffed her pillows. I took her wedding band from the beaded box and slipped it over her finger. It was 7 p.m. and dark.

The post-op instructions advised patients to sleep alone to protect their noses from thrashing arms, but we could not imagine being apart on this night. I placed a sleeping bag on my side of the bed and zipped myself in. Every few hours I'd get up to hand my fitfully sleeping spouse more ice packs, pills, water.

We'd been in bed almost twelve hours when a gray light filled the room. Still under our covers, we were warm and safe. Soon enough, we would face the world. I pulled my right arm from the sleeping bag and took my partner's hand. We stayed like that, side by side, until the sun rose on our first day in this foreign land.

Diane Daniel lives with her wife in Eindhoven, the Netherlands. Find her at shewasthemanofmydreams.com. This essay appeared in August 2011.

FAMILY MATTERS

SOMETHING LIKE MOTHERHOOD

CAROLYN MEGAN

I'M DRIVING MY NIECE AND NEPHEW TO THE MU-seum of Science. At the end of our outing, when I take them home, their father—my brother John—will tell them that their mother's latest cancer treatment has failed and that she will die. But for now, my niece, who's nine, rifles through my glove compartment and discovers a tampon. She tears open the wrapper, ejects the tampon, and begins swinging it by the string.

"What's this?"

"It's a tampon," I say.

"What's it for?"

It seems like a loaded question. To understand tampons means first understanding menstruation, which means understanding the whole life cycle. I have no idea what John and my sister-in-law, Sarah, have told her up to this point. "Well, you know how babies are made, right?"

"No," she says.

My nephew, thirteen, who is playing with his Game Boy in the backseat, says: "Oh, boy. Here we go."

"What?" she says, sitting upright.

How should I respond? I don't want my niece to feel awkward about her sexuality, and anyway I want John to have the opportunity to discuss this with her himself. I begin to talk around the edges but pause as I approach a toll booth, at which point my niece drops the tampon and reaches for the radio dial. I'm off the hook.

Later, when I tell John about the conversation, he replies, "I can't tell her what it is to be a woman. You'll probably be the one who helps her with all of this."

I realize he's probably right. Over the past eighteen months, as Sarah's condition has worsened, I've assumed more than a few parental duties. I've driven to my niece's and nephew's soccer games, attended school events, gone to pediatric appointments. I've lain awake at night rubbing their backs, tried to relearn algebra, studied the Civil War, bought McDonald's, nixed Chuck E. Cheese's, doled out medicines, done loads of laundry, said no more times than I've felt comfortable, said yes more times than I've felt comfortable.

During this time I've found myself moving into situations with a calm parent-like demeanor while admitting on the inside that I have no idea what I'm doing.

After delivering the children to John and Sarah at their house, I wait outside the room where they meet. The plan is that John and Sarah will tell the kids together and that I will then enter to be with them as they process the news. When John opens the door, he whispers, "They're devastated. They want you to come in, but they don't want to talk."

I walk into a tableau of shock and grief. Sarah sits on the couch, half asleep under the influence of pain killers, resting her hand on my niece, who is sobbing. My nephew cries and walks around the room with his arms crossed in front of his body, so much the body language of a teenager now.

I walk over and hug him; he leans up against me, letting out stifled sobs, his arms still crossed. In that moment some part of my heart opens and a new love pours out, not a recalibration or reconfiguring of the love I have, but a new well tapped. No separation of myself with him. And in that moment I think: *I will do anything for you.*

But will I?

Early in Sarah's illness, when John was already imagining a world without her, he asked whether my partner, Michael, and I would consider moving in with them. "You won't have to do anything. It would be just to have you there as a presence in the house."

I never answered him. I said things like "We'll see how this unfolds" or "Don't go there yet." Stall tactics. Each time he asked, I felt trapped, an impending sense of desperation and doom. It's the same feeling I had years ago that led to my decision not to have children.

The decision came from my desire to be fully in my life as a writer rather than to raise a child. Having a child was not how I wanted to make meaning of my life, not how I wanted to give back to the world. And the reason for this was my sense that I would love too fiercely, too desperately, at the cost of my *self.*

I knew my children would always come first and my art second, and I sensed the resentment I would feel about that. So I made a choice and said no to the idea of a child. But my niece and nephew are alive and here and need taking care of now. And I have stepped in without hesitation, something I could never regret.

Yet the very concern that informed my decision not to have children has come true: all my energy, love, and passion are focused on my niece and nephew, and I mourn the loss of a part of myself that has been pushed aside. In essence John's question of whether I might move in leaves me once again choosing whether or not I want to have children.

When I'm out with my niece and nephew, strangers already assume I'm their mother. I ask the sales clerk at a clothing store where the kids' T-shirts are, and she asks, "How old is your daughter?"

"Nine," I say. She points me to the girls' section, where there are a number of shirts trimmed with flowers.

"I might have better luck in the boys' section," I tell her. "She's a tomboy and would much prefer a soccer shirt."

The clerk laughs. "Oh, one of those."

It's so easy to slip into this role, so comfortable. Easier than explaining my not having kids to people who inquire. Easier than having to assure others that I love kids and that my decision isn't a reflection of a troubled childhood, not an act of selfishness. It is simply a choice. But in that moment with the sales clerk, I experience the ease of being in the mainstream, and it is a relief. This scene repeats itself: hugging my niece and nephew when they come off the soccer field, waiting for them at the bus stop, hearing my niece yell as she runs in from playing outside, "Mom! We need a drink!" When she finds me in the kitchen, she laughs and says, "I mean, Aunt Carolyn."

Anyone observing us would assume I am their mother. But I'm not and don't want to be. Yet given all that has happened, how can I not be?

People have always had their own ideas about why I don't have children: "Was it the divorce?" "Never found the right person at the right time?" "Biological clock?"

Now the story has a more positive spin: "Isn't it amazing how things work out?" "You didn't have kids, and now you can be there for your niece and nephew." "It's like it was meant to be."

Literature is rife with spinster aunts who move in with families when a sibling or in-law dies. They care for the ill parent and stand vigil until death. They step in and become surrogate mothers, platonic "wives" who efficiently take over the ministrations of the household and children.

There is an expectation of sacrifice: your life, your story, for the sake of the new story unfolding.

I'd like to believe that I don't need to be present all the time in order to be a mother figure to my niece and nephew. I'd like to believe that knowing they are loved and nurtured, whether I am there every day or not, will shore them up and give them the grounding they need to move healthfully into their adult lives.

But the day-to-day concerns pull at me. My nephew has athlete's foot. Under his littlest toe there is a large crack that he insists is from scraping the toe on a pool. A small matter, really, except that my brother hasn't had the chance to buy foot ointment.

Other worries: clean clothes, the lice outbreak at school.

Why is my niece's friend teasing her? Has anyone talked to my nephew about wet dreams? Is it okay that he shuts his bedroom door to be alone? Is there any vegetable that they'll eat? Are they having too much sugar? Of course John worries about these things, but he is exhausted. And the toilet is broken, the dryer has a squeaking sound, the dog is limping, there's no milk for tomorrow morning's cereal.

And then there is the meeting for parents whose children are in the school production of *The Hobbit*. My nephew is one of the dwarfs, and this meeting is to discuss the logistics and who will have the coveted roles of stage manager, prop master, and costume designer. There are only women present.

They talk about last year's production, laugh, and claim intimacy with one another and the process of putting on a show.

"We need to discuss how to get the working parents involved," one of the organizers says. The others nod in agreement. "This needs to be a community event."

I am there because I don't want my nephew to feel as though he doesn't have someone supporting him. I'm there because a friend of mine, whose mother died when she was young, once told me that she always felt like an orphan being fobbed off onto various caretakers. I don't want my nephew to feel like an orphan.

Yet I feel like an imposter, an outsider. I couldn't care less about the power struggle for who will be the stage manager. I am bored. I'd rather be home and am anxious to get back to my writing.

But I find being away from the kids a continual ache and worry.

I wonder how they are and miss being near them, touching them. I'm interested in their stories, in the young people they are becoming.

And although I am not a mother and never will be, this pull feels like it must be a kind of motherhood: as difficult as I expected, yes, but also full of wonder.

Carolyn Megan writes and teaches in Portland, Maine, and can be contacted at mainewritingworkshop@gmail.com. This essay appeared in September 2005.

FIRST I MET MY CHILDREN, THEN MY GIRLFRIEND. THEY'RE RELATED.

AARON LONG

I DIDN'T MEET MY GIRLFRIEND, JESSICA, UNTIL twelve years after our daughter, Alice, was born.

Let me explain. Nearly twenty-five years ago, I returned from a year of teaching English abroad, moved in with my mother, and, lacking prospects, began driving a cab. One day I saw a newspaper ad seeking healthy men, eighteen to thirty-five, to participate in a semen donation program.

Donors is the standard industry word, yet virtually all of us are paid. Forty dollars a pop was what I received in 1994.

I applied to sell my sperm and sold twice weekly for a year. At the time I was in a long-distance relationship, so this seemed like a good outlet. When I told my mother, she presciently wondered aloud if this was the only way she was going to have grandchildren.

Today, sperm buyers view detailed profiles for potential vendors, whereas I wasn't asked to provide much beyond college major, hobbies, and family health history. Jessica and her partner at the time chose me primarily because I was a writer and musician.

After a year of selling my sperm, I went back to giving it away and largely forgot about the whole thing. Occasionally the subject of whether I had children would come up, and I'd make a joke about probably having a bunch. I had signed a nondisclosure waiver and assumed there would never be a way for my progeny and me to find one another.

Then the Internet happened.

In the early 2000s, I searched online for a way to find my offspring and discovered the Donor Sibling Registry but didn't see any leads there and never got around to checking back. (I had looked way too early: My progeny began to use the site to find each other when they became teenagers in the 2010s.)

A couple of years ago I began seeing ads for 23andMe, a service that analyzes your saliva—you spit in a test tube and mail it off for analysis—and provides you with information about ancestry, health, and DNA relatives. The opportunity was obvious, but I assumed the odds of finding my children were low. I procrastinated for months before curiosity and an urge to know them made me order a kit.

I got my results back, and boom: I had a son, Bryce. His full name was unusual enough that I easily Googled him, and the picture resembled me enough that I felt confident this senior geography major was mine (mine?). Guessing he had been notified of my existence by 23andMe, I mulled in agitation for a week before finally putting fingers to keyboard.

"Dear Bryce," I wrote. "I recently joined 23andMe and

found you listed as my 'son,' so I believe myself to be your biological father. I hope my existence isn't a shock and wonder whether you joined in hopes of connecting with me." My letter continued awkwardly from there, giving him a brief sketch of my life.

Bryce replied almost instantly: "Dad, I cannot express how excited I am to be hearing from you. I did join 23andMe hoping that you would have already done so and was upset to see you hadn't. This is amazing though and I'm so happy. I'm one of six of your children that I'm aware of and in contact with. I'm 20 years old and live on Long Island but I'm studying in upstate New York."

"Dad?" I was briefly concerned that Bryce might have some fatherly expectations of me and show up on my doorstep, but my worries were unfounded. It's a brave new world, and we're all struggling with the terminology.

More important, six children? Yikes! I did some napkin math based on the number of samples I provided and the odds of conception and estimated that I may have as many as 67 children.

Bryce connected me with Madalyn, nineteen. Upon viewing her Facebook page, I had my first parental thought ever: My daughter should put some more clothes on.

I may be biased, but I found my children to be ridiculously attractive. I felt a sudden need to share their photos with all the ex-girlfriends who chose not to marry and procreate with me.

A few months later a new DNA relative appeared on 23andMe: Alice, age eleven. Her mother, Jessica, wrote me a note. She and her former partner had each given birth to one daughter conceived with my sperm. They broke up years ago but had been raising both girls together until recently, when the other mother moved away with the daughter she had given birth to.

Jess and I began to chat online. She knew a lot about buying sperm and self-impregnating, which was fascinating for me to learn, and, it turns out, more difficult than my role: masturbating into a cup. She also no longer identified as lesbian and was dating a man who, incredibly, had my same first and middle names (Aaron David), with a similar, monosyllabic last name.

Had there been a mix-up at the Bureau of Boyfriends? Was I the one who was supposed to be dating her?

My children and I exchanged written biographies. Bryce's showed me how little I know of young adult culture and reminded me that one's twenties are a difficult decade. Madi's revealed a keen understanding of her upbringing and the parts of it she would like to break from. But it was Alice's, entitled "A series of awkward events separated by snacks," that floored me.

Hers was a hodgepodge of lists and memories written under duress ("Mom: Write or death!"). Favorite color: "Black. Like my soul." Favorite holiday: "Halloween (because candy and murder)." She liked Alfred Hitchcock films. "Basically," she wrote, "I'm an angsty teen in a child's body."

This kid's eleven?

A plan developed for Bryce and Madi to come to Seattle for a couple of weeks in the summer. Jess and Alice lived a few hours south and would drive up. I figured meeting my children was going to be the closest thing I'd ever have to a wedding, so I decided to host a party.

I had told my news to a few people, but most learned of

it from the "Meet My Kids Party" Facebook invitation, featuring photos of Bryce, Madi, and Alice. The shock value was high.

Be it genetics, good luck, or force of circumstance, I loved my children right away. They have an uncanny aura of me-ness. Bryce is shy but sharp and obsessed with memes in a way I might have been had I grown up Gen Z. Alice has little use for adults, as I still don't. Madi, especially, has my sense of humor and eyes: Locking gazes with her makes my brain explode, but then we laugh.

At the party, we played a nature-versus-nurture question-and-answer game and discovered we were all quite liberal and that none of us believed in God. None of them, however, sleeps with a pillow between their knees, as I have long done.

The first time Jess and I found ourselves alone we hugged at length in a way entirely inappropriate for people who had just met. Jess says I have mannerisms that remind her of both of her daughters and thus felt instantly comfortable with me.

Whether we were pawns of fate or unwitting participants in a chromosomally arranged marriage, Jess and I quickly bonded. I deployed my Bureau of Boyfriends mix-up line to a grudging but sweet reception. During the vacation, she and I fell easily into the mom-and-dad role for Bryce, Madi, and Alice. We soon had in-jokes and teased each other about our foibles, just like any family. I even gave Bryce and Madi a lecture about smoking.

At the end of the visit, Bryce somehow managed to get Jess and Alice kicked out of the house they were renting by climbing onto the roof to retrieve a toy, so I invited them to stay with me while they figured things out. What Jess soon figured out was that she wanted to keep staying with me. Alice rolled her eyes as if she had been tricked into a traditional family arrangement.

While 23andMe is not generally considered a dating site, Jess and I are grateful to the technology that has made our backward-formed relationship possible. We have a lot of questions about love and genetics and whether we would have felt this connection had we met in a more conventional way.

Our bond has survived the "How cool is this?" phase, though we still enjoy cybermonitoring my other progeny and speculating about how many more may emerge. (I'm up to ten now; I have had some contact with the new ones' mothers but haven't made plans to meet yet.)

Madi liked the West Coast and us and recently moved into our place. We're hoping to lure Bryce back, too.

In the end, the sci-fi trappings of our love story are irrelevant: Jess and I work as a couple because we like spending time together. I suppose it doesn't hurt that I happen to be the father of her child.

Aaron Long is a writer in Seattle. This essay was published in September 2018.

WHEN MR. RELIABLE BECOMES MR. NEEDY

KATHERINE TANNEY

MY MOTHER LIVED A SHORT DRIVE FROM THE nursing home where, early last year, my father died. Yet she was not with him at the end, nor did she know that her three daughters were in town, gathered around his bedside. As his ability to draw breath slowly ebbed, it is probable that she was at home watching HBO, reading a novel, or fixing herself a snack. They were married forty-seven years—"all wonderful," to quote my mother, who apparently wasn't counting the last five, when her husband, at sixty-three, became ill with Alzheimer's, her world disintegrated, and nothing between them was ever wonderful again.

That's the ending. Concise, cold. Yet what does an ending say, really, about a life, a marriage? My mother's complaints began six years ago, when she told my sisters and me over the phone that our father was being "mean" to her and "impossible to deal with." He left the burner on in the kitchen. He needed help figuring out which end of his shirt to pull over his head. At 2:00 a.m., he shaved and dressed, then went to the curb for the morning paper, waking my mother to complain when it wasn't there. Worst of all, she said, was his stubborn insistence that nothing was the matter with him.

It is not hard for me to imagine their arguments during this period. My mother always reacted to things that frightened her by going on the attack or running away, and my father could be quite stubborn, even vindictive. The thing was, when my sisters and I observed our father firsthand, we saw none of the paranoia or belligerence she described. To us, he simply appeared a lot needier than before, more forgetful, and disconcertingly unaware that his perceptions no longer corresponded to reality.

It should be said that "needy" and "impossible" always had been my mother's signature traits, while my father was Mr. Reliable, Mr. Self-Control. He calmly took us to McDonald's on nights she was too busy slamming doors or breaking beloved objects to prepare dinner. On other occasions, when we went out as a family, he dutifully came around the car to open her door and gave the waiter her order as she sat and posed.

"The lady will have . . ." he always began.

My parents had big plans for their golden years, plans they both understood from the earliest days of their marriage. My father was tall and handsome, watchful and quiet, from a broken, modest home. My mother was outspoken and creative, furious and impulsive, from a wealthy, accomplished family. The longer they stayed married, the closer they came to her inheritance and their helium dreams of owning a retirement home in Aspen or a pied-à-terre in Paris or Manhattan. This is what my parents were about. They believed that money was for the exclusive purpose of giving themselves pleasurable experiences. Rarely did they contribute to charities, political causes, or even to the public television and radio stations they enjoyed. Their money supported pricey restaurants and performing arts box offices, makers of costly apparel, home furnishings, fine art, and fancy cars.

But then the Alzheimer's was diagnosed, which had not been in my mother's plan, and her response was to shut down. To our suggestion that she find a support group, she said, "I called. It's for widows, not people with living spouses."

To our recommendation that she find a therapist, she complained, "If they really cared, they wouldn't charge."

When we urged her to get someone to help her out, she said, "I can't have strangers in my house."

Rather than educate herself about the disease and how to handle it, she assigned my father chores to complete in the garden and around the house, as though disciplined work could restore order to their lives. Instead he'd wander away, get on a bus—he had lost his driving privileges by then—and turn up hours later in a cab, leaving the clueless driver to deal with my mother's foul state.

Those were the final days for them, when the flood of loving words my mother issued for her husband were in sobbing past tense, as though he had already passed away. The man she was living with she considered a stranger she had to drive to the doctor and keep a constant eye on, but with whom a good conversation was no longer possible.

I often wondered how other spouses coped. Magazines were full of articles about couples dealing heroically with Alzheimer's, families coming together to care for the afflicted member. *You and me against the world.* How many marriages are based on some form of this sentiment, and what happens when the world unexpectedly scores a coup?

My father, who had always defended the worst of my mother's words and deeds, was now dependent upon the one who had depended upon him the most. In the absence of anyone my mother could blame for this betrayal, she blamed him. When my sisters and I learned from her that our father was roaming the city on foot without money or food or water, and that she refused to go get him when he called from pay phones in dangerous neighborhoods, lost and disoriented, it was finally agreed that for his own good he should be moved away from her.

So began my parents' separate journeys, still tumultuous because of my mother's increasingly erratic decision making. She developed an unprecedented fear of spending money that led to my father being moved six times in the final four and a half years of his life.

First he lived with my sister, who employed private help to attend to him when she was at work. When his condition worsened, we moved him to an assisted-living center, where his eventual incontinence triggered a rate hike my mother refused to pay. We found another place. Then, claiming she had come to the end of his money and citing a sudden desire to be with her beloved until the end, my mother announced her intention to discontinue paying again.

"I'm going to take care of him myself," she said. He'd been gone almost three years by then, during which she'd seen him only twice, when he could still walk, still speak. Despite our objections and explanations about his advanced condition, she moved him back home, where he lasted only three days before he got hurt, forcing her to call 911.

"I wash my hands of him," she told the hospital social worker on the phone. "I'm not paying another penny."

There are many things I've left out: walks my orphaned father and I shared; laughs we had; the entrance of lawyers into our lives, with their legalese and bills; the volley of angry communications between mother and daughters; scenes from the homes where Alzheimer's patients live together in a cuckoo's nest of monotony. I gave my father a big stuffed animal with a bell in its tail. He liked the feel of the fur under his fingers. I bought him a ball, and we played catch, which he was exceptionally good at. He enjoyed being touched and talked to.

At approximately the same time that my mother washed her hands of my father, she came into her inheritance. After his death, she continued to live in their five-bedroom, split-level canyon home, complete with deck, hot tub, and state-of-the-art kitchen. The kind of architecturally interesting house you might see in a magazine, all right angles and vertical thrust, it was worth more than a million dollars. Somewhere in that house, presumably in a tasteful urn, she kept my father's ashes. My sisters and I had paid the crematorium bill, but when my mother found out about his death she insisted on paying what was owed and keeping his ashes with her. After all, it was his trouble she couldn't deal with, and now that he was no longer trouble she wanted him back.

I was not on speaking terms with my mother when my

father died, and neither were my sisters. In a message she left me after he went, she told me I would die "alone and penniless"—for abandoning her, I presume, just as she had abandoned my father. And then, six months later, right before she was scheduled for bypass surgery, my mother had a heart attack.

I took my time getting out to see her, partly because she was unconscious and not expected to pull through and partly because I suspected my presence would offer little in the way of comfort. But when I finally got there, the sight of my mother—every bit as helpless and desiccated as my father had been—rendered the past newly irrelevant, and we ended our years of discord on a grace note. She died five weeks later.

It is hard for me to accept this wrenching example of familial dissolution handed to me midway through my own bumpy life. What is the moral? Who is the villain? Shouldn't we all, after so many years with my mother, have known what she was and wasn't capable of? And is it possible my father might have condoned her behavior, or at least forgiven it, if he'd been able to think straight? "Shoot me now," I imagine him saying at the outset, had he been able to see what was coming and what it would cost.

Did my parents have a "wonderful" marriage? Of course they didn't. Nor was it so bad. They had a marriage. My father had a death. It should have been better, but such is the nature of survival and love. Last week, one of my dogs found a weakling of a bird in the grass and killed it slowly, expertly prolonging its life to keep it a toy for as long as possible. Watching through the window, I was torn apart and enlightened.

I used to think the final moment of life was the moment of truth, and I worried about it. I attempted bizarre feats of imagination, such as trying to will my own death during a moment of exquisite happiness. "Now," I coaxed the universe, my eyes shut, my breath on hold, "take me now." Because I knew all too well what tends to follow exquisite happiness, and I desperately wanted the universe to make an exception for me.

Katherine Tanney is the author of the novel Carousel of Progress. *This essay appeared in February 2005.*

MY FIRST LESSON
IN MOTHERHOOD

ELIZABETH FITZSIMONS

I SAW THE SCAR THE FIRST TIME I CHANGED NATalie's diaper, just an hour after the orphanage director handed her to me in a hotel banquet room in Nanchang, a provincial capital in southeastern China.

Despite the high heat and humidity, her caretakers had dressed her in two layers, and when I peeled back her sweaty clothes I found the worst diaper rash I'd ever seen, and a two-inch scar at the base of her spine cutting through the red bumps and peeling skin.

The next day, when the Chinese government would complete the adoption, also was Natalie's first birthday. We had a party for her that night, attended by families we'd met and representatives of the adoption agency, and Natalie licked cake frosting from my finger. But we worried about a rattle in her chest, and there was the scar, so afterward my husband, Matt, asked our adoption agency to send the doctor.

We had other concerns, too. Natalie was thin and pale and couldn't sit up or hold a bottle. She had only two teeth, and barely any hair, and wouldn't smile. But I had anticipated such things. My sister and two brothers were adopted from Nicaragua, the boys as infants, and when they came home they were smelly, scabies-covered diarrhea machines who could barely hold their heads up. Yet those problems soon disappeared.

I believed Natalie would be fine, too. There was clearly a light on behind those big dark eyes. She rested her head against my chest in the baby carrier and would stare up at my face, her lips parting as she leaned back, as if she knew she was now safe.

She would be our first child. We had set our hearts on adopting a baby girl from China years before, when I was reporting a newspaper story about a local mayor's return home with her new Chinese daughter. Adopting would come later, we thought. After I became pregnant.

But I didn't become pregnant. And after two years of trying, I was tired of feeling hopeless, of trudging down this path not knowing how it would end. I did know, however, how adopting would end: with a baby.

So we'd go to China first and then try to have a biological child. We embarked on a process, lasting months, of preparing our application and opening our life to scrutiny until one day we had a picture of our daughter on our refrigerator. Fourteen months after deciding to adopt, we were in China.

And now we were in a hotel room with a Chinese doctor,

an older man who spoke broken English. After listening to Natalie's chest, he said she had bronchitis. Then he turned her over and looked at her scar.

Frowning, he asked for a cotton swab and soap. He coated an end in soap and probed her sphincter, which he then said was "loose." He suspected she'd had a tumor removed and wondered aloud if she had spina bifida before finally saying that she would need to be seen at the hospital.

Two taxis took us all there, and as we waited to hear news, I tried to think positive thoughts: of the room we had painted for Natalie in light yellow and the crib with Winnie-the-Pooh sheets. But my mind shifted when I saw one of the women from the agency in a heated exchange in Chinese with the doctors, then with someone on her cellphone. We pleaded with her for information.

"It's not good," she said.

A CT scan confirmed that there had been a tumor that someone, somewhere, had removed. It had been a sloppy job; nerves were damaged, and as Natalie grew her condition would worsen, eventually leaving her paralyzed from the waist down. Control over her bladder and bowels would go, too; this had already begun, as indicated by her loose sphincter. Yes, she had a form of spina bifida, as well as a cyst on her spine.

I looked at my husband in shock, waiting for him to tell me that I had misunderstood everything. But he only shook his head.

I held on to him and cried into his chest, angry that creating a family seemed so impossible for us, and that life had already been so difficult for Natalie.

Back at the hotel, we hounded the women from the

agency: Why wasn't this in her medical report? How could a scar that size not be noticed? It was two inches long, for God's sake.

They shook their heads. Shrugged. Apologized.

And then they offered a way to make it better.

"In cases like these, we can make a rematch with another baby," the one in charge said. The rest of the process would be expedited, and we would go home on schedule. We would simply leave with a different girl.

Months before, we had been presented with forms asking which disabilities would be acceptable in a prospective adoptee—what, in other words, did we think we could handle: HIV, hepatitis, blindness? We checked off a few mild problems that we knew could be swiftly corrected with proper medical care. As Matt had written on our application: "This will be our first child, and we feel we would need more experience to handle anything more serious."

Now we faced surgeries, wheelchairs, colostomy bags. I envisioned our home in San Diego with ramps leading to the doors. I saw our lives as being utterly devoted to her care. How would we ever manage?

Yet how could we leave her? Had I given birth to a child with these conditions, I wouldn't have left her in the hospital. Though a friend would later say, "Well, that's different," it wasn't to me.

I pictured myself boarding the plane with some faceless replacement child and then explaining to friends and family that she wasn't Natalie, that we had left Natalie in China because she was too damaged, that the deal had been a healthy baby and she wasn't.

How would I face myself? How would I ever forget? I would always wonder what happened to Natalie.

I knew this was my test, my life's worth distilled into a moment. I was shaking my head "No" before they finished explaining. We didn't want another baby, I told them. We wanted our baby, the one sleeping right over there. "She's our daughter," I said. "We love her."

Matt, who had been sitting on the bed, lifted his glasses and, wiping the tears from his eyes, nodded in agreement.

Yet we had a long, fraught night ahead, wondering how we would possibly cope. I called my mother in tears and told her the news.

There was a long pause. "Oh, honey."

I sobbed.

She waited until I'd caught my breath. "It would be OK if you came home without her."

"Why are you saying that?"

"I just wanted to absolve you. What do you want to do?"

"I want to take my baby and get out of here," I said.

"Good," my mother said. "Then that's what you should do."

In the morning, bleary-eyed and aching, we decided we would be happy with our decision. And we did feel happy. We told ourselves that excellent medical care might mitigate some of her worst afflictions. It was the best we could hope for.

But within two days of returning to San Diego—before we had even been able to take her to the pediatrician—things took yet another alarming turn.

While eating dinner in her high chair, Natalie had a

seizure—her head fell forward then snapped back, her eyes rolled, and her legs and arms shot out ramrod straight. I pulled her from the high chair, handed her to Matt, and called 911.

When the paramedics arrived, Natalie was alert and stable, but then she suffered a second seizure in the emergency room. We told the doctors what we had learned in China, and they ordered a CT scan of her brain.

Hours later, one of the emergency room doctors pulled up a chair and said gravely, "You must know something is wrong with her brain, right?"

We stared at her. Something was wrong with her brain, too, in addition to everything else?

"Well," she told us, "Natalie's brain is atrophic."

I fished into my purse for a pen as she compared Natalie's condition to Down syndrome, saying that a loving home can make all the difference. It was clear, she added, that we had that kind of home.

She left us, and I cradled Natalie, who was knocked out from seizure medicine. Her mouth was open, and I leaned down, breathing in her sweet breath that smelled like soy formula.

Would we ever be able to speak to each other? Would she tell me her secrets? Laugh with me?

Whatever the case, I would love her and she would know it. And that would have to be enough. I thanked God we hadn't left her.

She was admitted to the hospital, where we spent a fitful night at her bedside. In the morning, the chief of neurosurgery came in. When we asked him for news, he said, "It's easier if I show you."

In the radiology department screening room, pointing at the CT scan, he told us the emergency room doctor had erred; Natalie's brain wasn't atrophic. She was weak and had fallen behind developmentally, but she had hand-eye coordination and had watched him intently as he examined her. He'd need an MRI for a better diagnosis. We asked him to take images of Natalie's spine, too.

He returned with more remarkable news. The MRI ruled out the brain syndromes he was worried about. And nothing was wrong with Natalie's spine. She did not have spina bifida. She would not become paralyzed. He couldn't believe anyone could make such a diagnosis from the poor quality of the Chinese CT film. He conceded there probably had been a tumor, and that would need to be monitored, but she might be fine. The next year would tell.

There would be other scares, more seizures, and much physical therapy to teach her to sit, crawl, and walk. She took her first steps one day on the beach at twenty-one months, her belly full of fish tacos.

Now she is nearly three, with thick brown hair, gleaming teeth, and twinkling eyes. She takes swimming lessons, goes to day care, and insists on wearing flowered sandals to dance. I say to her, "Ohhhh, Natalie," and she answers, "Ohhhh, Mama." And I blink back happy tears.

Sometimes when I'm rocking her to sleep, I lean down and breathe in her breath, which now smells of bubble-gum toothpaste and the dinner I cooked for her while she sat in her high chair singing to the dog. And I am amazed that this little girl is mine.

It's tempting to think that our decision was validated by the fact that everything turned out OK. But for me that's not the point. Our decision was right because she was our daughter and we loved her. We would not have chosen the burdens we anticipated, and in fact we declared up front our inability to handle such burdens. But we are stronger than we thought.

Elizabeth Fitzsimons is vice president of leadership and engagement at the San Diego Regional Chamber of Commerce and its affiliate LEAD San Diego. A San Diego Library Commissioner and board member at the Jacobs & Cushman San Diego Food Bank, she lives with her husband, daughter, and twin sons in San Diego. This essay appeared in May 2007.

TWO MEN, BABY ON THE WAY, AND ME

REBECCA ECKLER

I WAS THREE MONTHS PREGNANT AND ENGAGED to be married when I met him. He and I were out for dinner with mutual friends. He made me laugh. He was very cute. And very single. He saw my ring and heard my announcement about the growing bump in my stomach. Nevertheless, he paid for my dinner and walked me home, and a couple of weeks later we made plans to go see an early movie.

After the movie, I invited him into my apartment and made him a vodka and orange juice. I drank water but felt first-date tipsy anyway.

Of course, it wasn't a date. How could it be, when I had a bump in my stomach and was engaged to the father of the bump? No, the word *date* was never uttered. I was in bed, alone, by ten. But before he left, this cute single man surveyed my apartment and told me I should have more secure locks on my sliding-glass doors. The next day, he dropped off a broomstick handle with my doorman, which I was to use to secure the sliding door in the back.

Where was my fiancé? He lived in a different city, thousands of miles away. We'd been together this way for years—apart, yes, but together. We saw each other once a month. Our arrangement was fine until I got pregnant, which had forced us to make decisions. We chose to get married (eventually) and live in his western city, but for me to remain for the duration of the pregnancy in my better-for-my-career eastern city, because it was, well, better for my career.

This confused many people. "Yes, I'm pregnant," I had to explain endlessly. "No, the fiancé is not here. Yes, I go to the obstetrician appointments by myself. Yes, he visits. Yes, I visit. Really, it's fine."

But now, inconveniently, I had met this new man who had brought me a broomstick for security. To friends, I started to refer to him as Broomstick. His other name was Cute Single Man.

Cute Single Man and I began to e-mail regularly. We played Scrabble. Soon we had a standing date on Thursday nights watching reality television. He would come to my apartment and bring me ice cream, sliced watermelon, and Big Macs, my craving foods.

When CSM and I went to Mr. Sub (another craving) late one Saturday night and the employee behind the counter asked us when we were due, it was easier to pretend he was the father than to explain that he was just a friend. After all, what kind of woman goes out with a cute single man at eleven on a Saturday night when she's pregnant with another man's child?

Also I didn't have a car, so CSM took me grocery shopping on Sunday afternoons. He carried the cases of bottled water. When we once shared an elevator with another pregnant couple, it was more natural for me to say, "We also can't wait for this thing to come out," than, "Well, I'm excited. I'm not sure he is. He's not the father."

When we went to the movies, people gazed at us with the warm approval generally bestowed upon pregnant couples. I suppose we looked wholesome and happy. And I couldn't help but think that he and I would have had a very good-looking baby.

At first, I thought CSM pitied me. Actually, I thought he was attracted to my big pregnant breasts. I was right in both instances.

After all, there I was, two cups larger than my pre-pregnant self, alone in a big city, pregnant, while the father was a four-hour plane ride away. But CSM shouldn't have pitied me. It was my choice.

CSM was becoming a version of the fill-in boyfriend, which many women in long-distance relationships have. The fill-in boyfriend takes you to the movies or to dinner, or sets up your DVD player. The only difference for us—besides the fact that I was pregnant and engaged—was that he was quickly becoming more than simply a version of the fill-in boyfriend.

"He's in love with you," my friend kept telling me. "Why is he attracted to an engaged pregnant woman? What's wrong with him? It's like you're the ultimate challenge."

Sometimes I did find his attraction odd, but like most women, I like to believe my personality is what attracts men. I didn't want to believe I was just a challenge or that he had commitment problems (though often I did think that). I also did not, or could not, believe that CSM was physically attracted to the pregnant me—in sweat pants, with cellulite on my arms and pimples on my chin.

Don't get me wrong. I wanted CSM to be attracted to me. I was pregnant, not dead. And I liked him, too. Very much, then too much, and then, yes, way too much. I would have said we were falling in love, but as it wasn't an appropriate time for me to be falling in love, I didn't say it. We certainly acted as if we were falling in love. I spoke to him first thing in the morning and at the end of every day. I missed him five minutes after he dropped me off. A night without seeing him felt like a month. He told me he had never cared for anyone like he cared for me.

And we fought like we were in a passionate relationship. One night I asked him to bring me chocolate ice cream. He brought me toffee-flavored instead. It was, I felt, the end of the world.

"Try it," he said. "You'll like it."

"I will not like it," I screamed. "I wanted chocolate ice cream. You never listen to me. It's always all about you!" I kicked him out of my house, like a madwoman. It was the pregnancy hormones.

I thought I had lost him forever that night, and I waited for hours by my perfectly functioning phone, wondering if it had been disconnected, hoping for him to call, and knowing it would be better if he didn't.

He did. I apologized. We made up.

Another time we went to a large party. I shouldn't have gone. I was six months pregnant by then, felt ugly and out of place, and needed a bathroom every five minutes. He refused to accompany me to the bathroom, asking why didn't I just find him afterward. He flirted with other women, or at least that's the way I saw it. And why shouldn't he have? We were at a party. It's not as if he were the father of my child.

I left the party without telling him, angry, jealous. He called me at 3:00 a.m., drunk and apologetic. I had to keep reminding myself he was not my fiancé, not the person I was going to marry and grow old with.

But when I had an obstetrician appointment, he would say, "Call me right after."

And I would. (Immediately after I called the fiancé.) I couldn't stop myself. My head was screaming, Stop! But my heart . . .

"It's a girl!" I told him. "I wanted a girl!"

"Fantastic!" he said.

Like the model expectant father, he loved placing his hand on my stomach when the baby kicked. "Wow," he'd say. "That's amazing."

He worried about me and about this baby that wasn't his. I worried what people would say about me if they knew about our relationship. He worried what people would say about him. I worried about my fiancé, whom I loved and didn't want to hurt and didn't want to lose. I worried about what the right thing was for my baby.

To the extent that we could, we kept "us" a secret. CSM did not tell his friends about me, and I told mine—those who knew—simply that I liked him and that he made me laugh.

But I knew we were crossing some line. If my fiancé were hanging out in his city with a cute single woman, I would have killed him. CSM never spoke of the fiancé, and I never spoke of CSM to the fiancé. If the fiancé suspected, he turned a blind eye. The denial! We were all swept up in it.

When I was very pregnant and it was time to leave CSM to be with the fiancé, my heart cracked. I cried on the plane. I no longer had any idea what I wanted. But I was having a baby in a few weeks. My life was about to change completely, and I was mostly wrapped up with the facts: I had gained forty-seven pounds, I could barely walk, and I was going to have an actual human thing to look after.

My baby is now no longer a baby. She is seventeen months old. Around the time my daughter was learning to walk, the supermodel Heidi Klum became engaged to Seal, after she met and dated him while pregnant with another man's child. No one, it seems, was bothered by this. Likewise, in the movie *The Life Aquatic with Steve Zissou,* the very pregnant journalist character ends up in bed with another man, not the father of her baby. Yet we all want her to be happy, and we're happy she hooks up with another man.

But I'm not sure anyone is happy about me and CSM. It's been more than two years since that fateful dinner and a year and a half since I moved away, yet he and I are still in touch. I take frequent trips to my eastern city, and we see each other. We struggle to figure out what, if anything, we are. We talk, we fight, we don't talk. He misses me. I miss him. He hates me. I hate him. On and on it goes.

The fiancé and I have struggled, too. We have not married. We have not regained that clarity. We ask ourselves, "Are we happy together?" "Are we meant to be?" Those are, and perhaps forever will be, our questions. Maybe they are everyone's questions.

And finally, of course, there are the "if onlys." If only I'd moved west to be with my fiancé at the start. If only I hadn't gone to that dinner. If only CSM and I hadn't met at such an inopportune time. If only we could plan falling in love like a scheduled C-section.

Rebecca Eckler lives in Toronto with her two children. Her latest book is Blissfully Blended Bullshit. *She is the executive editor of* SavvyMom. *This essay appeared in March 2005.*

WHEN MOM IS ON THE SCENT, AND RIGHT

LIZA MONROY

I DON'T LIKE HIM," MY MOTHER SAID. I HAD CALLED her from the train after visiting my long-distance boy-friend of eight months in Boston. I wanted to tell her how hard I had fallen for him, a man I had gone to college with but didn't know then. We met at our ten-year reunion and imme-diately connected. He was moving to Brooklyn to live with me. I was thrilled, but my mother insisted it was a mistake.

"You've never even met him," I said.

"I have negative vibes," she said.

"You've never even seen him."

"I don't like what he posts on Facebook."

"You've never had one conversation with him."

"He's not a bad person," she said. "He's just not right for you."

"You focus on such superficial qualities," I argued. "Snap judgments tell you nothing about a relationship."

"I'm a profiler. It's what I do for a living."

For twenty-six years my mother worked for the State Department as a consular officer in the Foreign Service, interviewing visa applicants, quickly determining whether they were lying about their plans, whether they would stay illegally.

"When you talk to several hundred people a day, you get good," she said. "It becomes second nature." She has won awards for her work, and she thought I should listen to her judgments of my romantic partners.

Instead, I became irate.

"You don't let other people embrace who they are," I said at the end of that train call. "And that's why being around you is suffocating."

Frustrated, I called my cousin Doug, who also had worked in the Foreign Service.

"It's a mathematical equation based on how your mother interviews visa applicants," he said. "She has it down to a science: What's his income, his job, his background? She's applying the same criteria to your relationships."

He was right. My mother was profiling my boyfriend based on, well, a profile: a half-sleeve tattoo and status updates. My boyfriend's rocker appearance and brief posts didn't represent the man who loved children and the ocean as much as I did, who was talented at baking and home repair.

He held a job at a prestigious university and worked on films in his spare time. He was kind and loving. I didn't understand what my mother saw as wrong. I suspected she would have approved were he exactly the same but Jewish and sans tattoo and band T-shirts.

At thirty-two, I didn't want her input on my every decision. How could she really know? Her job kept her overseas
and we saw each other about twice a year. While she jok-
ingly called herself "the Profiler," I called her by some other
names: "MicroMOMager" and "Smother."

I was starting to think she would find a reason any man
I dated wasn't right. I was her only child. What if, I began to
suspect, she didn't want me to find someone so she could
keep me for herself?

What really worried me, though, was that she had done
this before and been right.

My previous relationship was with a poet I met in graduate school. Within a month, we planned to move to some
quaint college town where we would fill our life with books,
pets, and elaborate vegetarian meals. My childhood spent
moving around the world with my mother instilled in me a
desire for a more rooted, traditional family. I thought I had
found a compatible man.

Then the Profiler swooped in from Venezuela.

"I don't like him," she announced after five minutes in a
restaurant. He had gone to the restroom. "Something's off."

I ignored her.

Three years later, though, I discovered the poet had
been lying for months to conceal a dire financial circumstance. I believed I could no longer trust him. We went to
therapy. I asked him to move out.

Some nights later, I came home to find he had slashed
my clothes, put my two laptops in the bathtub, and destroyed
some family photographs—some of the only ones I had of
my father, who had died. I was shocked that he was capable
of being so destructive.

I called the Profiler from family court, where the police instructed I go to get an order of protection.

"Something was off," I said. "You have to approve anyone I'm thinking about getting serious with."

We joked that it would make a good romantic-comedy premise.

She tried her best to change my mind about the Boston filmmaker, but he was already moving his editing equipment into my one-bedroom apartment in Brooklyn.

My mother finally met him when she visited from Spain. "He's nice," she conceded. "But not right for you. I wish you weren't moving in together."

"Maybe you don't want me to be in a relationship because you don't have one," I snapped.

It was harsh, but it seemed to me that my very existence as the daughter of a single mother was proof of her questionable judgment in men. If she couldn't profile for herself, how could she do it for me?

My parents met on a ship. She was a PhD student in Italy, and he the charismatic maître d'hôtel in the ship's restaurant. They were together three months when he was denied a tourist visa to the United States, so they married. Gradually, though, my father fell prey to alcoholism, and they divorced when I was six.

I asked her why she thought she could discern from a photograph who wasn't right for me when she picked the worst men for herself.

"That's a good question," she said. "I have no idea." She paused. "You fool yourself. People over the whole course of history have probably had that problem."

I was committed to making it work with the filmmaker,

but a year later I began to acknowledge a nagging feeling that it wasn't quite right. I told him, and we parted amicably. It was a better breakup, no police. And we lived together peacefully for another month before he moved out.

"He's nice," my mother said. "But he wasn't the one."

The Profiler, right again. After the relationship was over and I could see clearly, I didn't like what he posted on Facebook, either.

"You don't see these things quickly like I do," my mother said. "You spend years with these people. The poet was worth two dates. And the filmmaker shouldn't have been moving in."

I might have been able to see these things, too; I just didn't want to. The poet had arrived drunk to pick me up for one of our early dates. Instead of asking him to leave, I brought him water and made him promise not to show up drunk again. I had already built up the fantasy of our idealized life and didn't want to ruin it.

When the filmmaker complained about hating his day job and being unsure how to pursue his dream, I didn't want to see that he needed to figure it out on his own.

I ignored my own profiling "power" for the same reason my mother didn't profile her boyfriends: I wanted to be in love, and love wasn't logical. I sought out men who were still finding themselves, hoping I could help them, a classic addict's child pattern. I couldn't save my father, who died from liver failure. And I couldn't fix any of these men's lives either.

Might I have avoided heartache by heeding my mother's advice? After all, she was right both times. But a relationship that doesn't work out isn't a waste. There is no exact science or crystal ball. Profiling is a surface art; real love isn't. As Hemingway once said, "The best way to find out if you can trust somebody is to trust them." Likewise, the best way to know if you are meant to be with someone is to be with him.

"We learn through making our own mistakes," I told her. "You should know."

She always said she never regretted marrying my father because she had me.

Now, we are both single. She retired from the Foreign Service to take care of my grandmother in Seattle, but she will always be the Profiler. Rather than letting it upset me, though, we've invented a more fun alternative: the Profiler Game, in which I show her Facebook pages of men I'm interested in, and she offers her professional evaluation.

I recently met a successful author at an event. We shared the quirk of being passionately into backgammon. When we reconvened the next afternoon to play, he leaned over the board and kissed me. Convinced this was something, I sent the Profiler to his reading in Seattle.

"I'd be much more pleased than with the other ones," she reported back. "He's Jewish and smart, and he'd be good for you because he's not good for someone taller."

Alas, the author was seeing someone else. Was the Profiler wrong? Had she finally missed? She suggested I go back on JDate.

"I'll do it if you do," I said.

Liza Monroy is the author of the memoirs The Marriage Act *and* Seeing as Your Shoes Are Soon to Be on Fire, *both of which originated as "Modern Love" essays. She lives and writes in Santa Cruz, California. This essay appeared in July 2012.*

TWO DECEMBERS: LOSS AND REDEMPTION

ANNE MARIE FELD

O N THE AFTERNOON MY MOTHER DIED, SHE LEFT work early. Her day as a computer programmer at Chase Manhattan Bank had skidded to an abrupt stop courtesy of a systemwide computer failure, and all the employees got the afternoon off. It was late December. My sixteenth birthday. Gray, snowless, cold enough to make the lawn crunch underfoot, but close enough to Christmas to make a few uncrowded hours seem like a gift. Or in my mother's case, a curse.

Rather than enjoying some last-minute shopping or hitting the couch, she methodically cleared her desk, drove the Honda home, fired up a pot of Turkish coffee, and hanged herself in our garage.

Twenty years later my father insists that she wouldn't have died that day if the systems hadn't gone down. He might be right. Work gave my mother a structure that sealed the madness inside, if only for small chunks of time. Idleness brought trouble.

My memories of my mother all have her working at something: cooking, staying up all night scraping wallpaper, poring over fat textbooks to get her master's degree. In home movies my sister and I, long-limbed and small-bodied, dance and do gymnastics in the foreground while my mother lurks in the background, washing dishes or zooming diagonally through the frame on her way somewhere else.

Though my mother worked full time, my sister and I never lifted a finger in that house. It was spotless, without the piles of clutter and tides of dust that mark my own house.

My mother's madness seeped in so quietly that my father, an optimist to the end, was able to ignore it, believing that it would get better on its own. In our house, questions about what we did and how we felt went unasked. Or if asked, unanswered. My sister and I ate alone in our bedrooms beside flickering black-and-white televisions.

I wasn't told about my mother's two earlier attempts at suicide and would never have guessed. In my mind, suicidal people raved and ranted. Madwomen were locked in attics, where they would moan and rattle chains. Occasionally they set fire to country estates. They certainly weren't grocery shopping or dropping the kids off at the community pool on their way to the office.

From fielding calls on the yellow rotary-dial phone in the kitchen, I knew that my mother saw a therapist, a woman named Barbara, whom she tried to pawn off as a friend. I knew better. My mother didn't have friends.

When I was fourteen, my mother started sleeping on the living room floor and wearing a dark gray ski hat with three white stripes. She seemed to drink nothing but gritty coffee and red wine poured from gallon bottles stored under the kitchen sink. She would send me into the pizzeria to pick up our pie, convinced that the men spinning crusts were talking about her behind her back.

As I limped along in my teenage bubble, very little of this registered as alarming. This was how all families were. As my mother's madness amplified, she came to believe that our house was bugged and that her boss was trying to hurt her. But as long as there was a computer program to write or a carpet to vacuum, she could be counted on to do it and do it well.

In her insistence upon getting things done, on living an ordered life, my mother managed to miss out on the nourishing aspects of family life and life in general: laughing at silly things, lying spooned on the couch with your beloveds, sharing good food, the tactile delight of giggling children crawling all over you. Without this, family life is an endless series of menial tasks: counters and noses to wipe, dishes and bodies to wash, whites and colors to fold, again and again in soul-sucking succession.

On the morning of the day my mother died, I headed toward the door to catch the 7:10 bus to school. My mother and twelve-year-old sister were just waking up in their sleeping spot on the gray carpet in the living room. They sang "Happy Birthday" to me, my mother's beautiful, low singing voice frosted with my sister's tinny soprano.

Eight hours later I stepped off the Bluebird bus, looking forward to an afternoon of *One Life to Live* and *All My Chil-*

dren, and was disappointed to see my mother's car in the driveway. I dropped my knapsack on the window seat, stroked the dog's dusty ears, and called, "Mommy?"

Her purse sat on the table. I checked all the rooms but found them empty. Then I opened the door to the garage and stopped breathing.

I shut the door, ran up the stairs and outside, and sat on the cold concrete stoop, looking up the street. House after split-level house stretched along the curved road with one thing in common: no one was home. All of the parents in my neighborhood worked, and since I had taken the early bus home from school, the kids were still gone as well.

I sat hunched over my legs, arms circling my shins, as my heart slowed. Finally I stood up, opened the screen door, went back into the house, and dialed 911.

In the days that followed, my father, sister, and I sloshed through a sea of awkwardness. The wife of a friend of my father's bought me a dress to wear to the funeral, a maroon velvet Gunny Sax monstrosity with puffed sleeves and lace trim.

Regular funerals are hard enough; the funeral of a suicide tests even the most socially skilled. When all the robotic thank-you-for-comings had been finished, my sister tried to open the coffin when no one was looking. My father stopped her just as she was about to lift the lid. "I just wanted to see her," she explained, almost inaudibly.

Other details needed handling, providing my first, metallic taste of the kind of chores that come with adulthood. For the first time in my life, a formal party had been planned for my birthday at a local catering hall. The party favors—clear Lucite boxes filled with Hershey's Kisses, decorated with pink and silver hearts—sat in bags in the garage, waiting.

But there would be no party. I picked up the phone and said, over and over, "I'm sorry, my Sweet Sixteen is canceled." By the time I was done, cold sweat ran down my wrist, wetting my sleeve. I didn't cry.

On the day the party was to be held, I stood in Loehmann's with my father. My mother's dress for the occasion, a gray wool sheath with long sleeves, lay on the counter. The clerk told my father that the garment couldn't be returned. My father looked at the clerk and said very quietly, "But she died." They took the dress back.

And as soon as I could, I fled. First to college, then to a place as far from Long Island as I could manage: San Francisco. Every night I would shimmy into a short black dress, tights, and platform boots and belly up to small, scarred stages, staring at would-be Kurt Cobains or boys in porkpie hats wailing Louis Armstrong covers, or nodding my head to the beat as shaved-bald DJs spun in corners of warehouses while hundreds of people raved, shaking water bottles over their heads until the sun shot weak rays through dirty skylights.

My rent was $365. I had some savings; work seemed optional, as did stability. Over the next decade I would have ten apartments, thirteen jobs, and at least as many boyfriends. I met Dave at a film festival, while waiting in line to see a movie called *Better Than Sex*. We started seeing movies together, always picking films with *sex* in the title. Months after we had run out of movies about fornication with no signs of doing so ourselves, he finally kissed me under a lamppost outside his front door. I was wearing knee-high black leather boots. He was wearing sheepskin slippers.

He phoned every day. He listened. He smiled a lot. He told me I was beautiful. He made up rap songs about our love. He wanted to talk about everything, from politics to my period. He wanted children. He was, as my best friend's father said, "a good citizen."

We found a house together, a 1920s cottage on a street of Spanish Mediterranean houses in every color of the rainbow. We split the down payment fifty-fifty and started packing. Driving alone through a torrential downpour to sign the title for our house, I lost it. I didn't do stable.

I convinced myself that Dave was a con man planning an elaborate sting to separate me from my down payment. The year we had spent together was the setup for the graft. Now I was going to be out twenty-five thousand dollars and a boyfriend. It was a hop, skip, and a jump from there to standing at the side of the road, homeless and utterly alone, the victim of aiming too high.

My hands were shaking when I pulled up outside the title company. Dave was standing there, holding an umbrella, waiting to walk me the ten feet from the curb to the building. Eight months later, just back from our honeymoon, he carried me up our wonky front steps and across the threshold before collapsing from exertion on the blue sofa in our office. Another eight months after that, a plastic stick with a pink line told us that our remodeling plans were going to have to wait.

On my first visit, the ob-gyn calculated the baby's due date: my birthday. I was terrified that my day of personal infamy would be shared by the next generation of my family. Friends spun it beautifully: "It'll be healing. It'll give you back that day."

The contractions didn't hit hard until Christmas night, four days after I turned thirty-six. Fifty-six hours after the first tremors hit my abdomen, three hours after the epidural wore off, I pushed my daughter into the world.

I wasn't thinking about my mother. Or about my sister, who stayed at the head of the bed, cheering me on when I thought my body would rip in two. Or about Dave, who watched tearfully as Pascale poured out. I thought nothing, and just lay there, shocked by pain and exhaustion. But when they finally returned her raw, chickenlike body to me after bathing her, my first thought was that she looked like my mother.

Anne Marie Feld is a writer and an editor. She lives in Northern California with her husband, two children, and a cat-sized dog. Her work has appeared in the New York Times, *Edutopia, and numerous anthologies and on Netflix. Her first novel,* Grilled, *is available on Amazon and you can find her online at www.annemariefeld.net. This essay appeared in January 2006.*

BEYOND DIVORCE AND EVEN DEATH, A PROMISE KEPT

JENNIFER JUST

IT'S DONE: I'VE FINALLY FINISHED MOVING MY ex-husband's belongings back into the large, cluttered farmhouse we used to share. He won't be coming back, but his shirts once again weigh down the closet rack, his boxes of household gadgets and financial files clog the attic and basement, and the furniture that wouldn't fit into the house now fills the third bay of the car barn.

Three years ago our marriage was ending. Corey and I had "outgrown" each other, shorthand for the malaise that had entered our marriage and despite our best efforts wouldn't leave. We were still friends; we didn't have big fights. All in all we'd had a pretty good marriage, and so we'd spent a lot of time discussing the necessity of divorcing.

We had our boys to consider—Evan, nine, and Cameron, thirteen—along with eighteen years of shared memories. And the idea of living apart unsettled us. When you've lived most of your adult life with someone else, you don't know what you can and can't do on your own anymore, what you can and can't live without.

Neither of us, however, seemed able to muster enough imagination to see a happy future together. We were less husband and wife than tenants living in the same house.

Although we had a good partnership when it came to raising our children, we didn't share much of anything else and didn't want to. But when we did decide to end our marriage, we did so with one caveat.

One night, in discussing what might happen after the split, Corey and I found ourselves promising that we'd always watch each other's backs. He had an especially concrete reason to worry: he had multiple sclerosis. Although the disease had progressed slowly, its unpredictability meant he could slide further downhill at any time.

"Listen," I told him. "Worse comes to worst, we move you back here. You just come back."

I don't know why it was so easy for me to promise to hold a space for him in my life and for him to promise the same. Maybe we had decided we could keep some parts of our wedding vows after all.

When we finally did separate, Corey bought a little beach house twenty minutes away in West Haven, Connecticut, that seemed to say so much about what he wanted and what he'd chosen to leave behind. He'd always been a minimalist (in contrast with my penchant for cleaning out tag sales and relatives' attics), and his new place, a clean-lined Cape, reflected his aesthetic. It had few surfaces to crowd with family memorabilia, a lot of room for his books, and the view of the water he'd always wanted.

I was happy for him, and I was happy for me, too, that once again I could be my messy and complicated self without apology. Even the kids seemed happier. Now they reveled in the time he was carving out for them: entire weekends and weeknights when it was just him and the boys.

Last Fourth of July, Cameron, Evan, and I were on our way back from a trip to Long Island when we decided to call Corey. His beach had a spectacular view of our region's fireworks, an immense parabola of light running up and down the coasts of Connecticut and New York.

He was thrilled to hear from us; he was missing the boys, he said, and by coincidence was marinating way too much chicken. So we dropped by for dinner, and when darkness fell, we walked down to the beach for the show.

Instantly Corey and I fell into our old patterns with our sons, joking with them as we always had, making up stories, and laughing as we rarely did with anyone else.

But when the noise and light subsided, it was time to go home, which for us of course meant separate homes. We shared a history and children, but what we had did not quite add up to a marriage. And that was okay. That night we'd found a way of being together that worked for us and our kids.

The next Saturday, I dropped off the boys to spend a whole week with their dad, and then I took them again for dinner the next Monday night.

Wednesday was Parents' Day at the boys' camp, and Corey was supposed to join me there, but he never came. I figured something had come up and decided not to bother him. But when I got home, I found ten voice mail messages waiting. The first was from Corey's sister, crying, asking me to call her right away.

Corey's parents, I thought. Something's happened to his parents.

The second message, however, was from the West Haven Police, saying they needed to speak to me immediately. I didn't have to play any of the other messages. I never have.

Corey had died the morning before, alone in his little house, of a heart ailment no one knew he had.

In the sleepless nights that followed, questions tormented me: If we'd still been living in the same house, would I have been able to save him? Had divorce really been necessary? Might we have found a way back to our marriage after enough (too much) time being single?

I easily could have spent my waking hours obsessing over such questions, but I had to take care of our sons. And soon I realized I had to keep my promise to Corey.

True, I'd promised to move him back in with us if his health failed, but this wasn't exactly what I'd bargained for. For starters, in the original plan he was alive, and my agonized decisions about what to keep or toss were to have been his to make, he who never agonized about anything. Second, it was hard to know how much to bring back of a man I had begun to extricate from my life. I'd been unraveling the threads of our joined lives, but now I was faced with having to pick up some of those stitches and weave the tapestry back together.

Back up on the wall went the family photos I'd taken down when Corey moved out. I reserved one bookshelf for his books, so the boys would know what he read. His CDs, too, got their own shelf near the stereo. I felt I had to restore his presence in our house. How else to show that he was once here? That he is, in some measure, still here?

There are hours of videotape, and someday I will edit them. But will I tell our sons the true story of our life (there are uneasy harbingers of the demise of our marriage in certain exchanges on those tapes), or will I decide to create a more easily digested version? This, too, is up to me and me alone.

Moving him home also involved closing up his beach house, dealing with his financial accounts, tracking down the far-flung friends who had no way of knowing he was gone, and otherwise wiping his life clean.

I thought it would be easier to incorporate his life back into ours if I took him home gradually, in carloads, over a period of weeks. And it was good I took the time and did it alone, because while packing I found things he might have preferred to keep boxed up: evidence of the girlfriend he hadn't yet introduced to the boys, X-rated gifts from office pals.

Archivist that I am by nature, I considered each item for its possible historical value. Did it say anything significant about who Corey was? His girlfriend, after all, had been a big part of his life; it wasn't right to expunge all evidence of her existence.

Last month I made my final trip to Corey's house to clean it before the new owners took possession. I scrubbed the bathroom, the refrigerator, the floors, and the walls with an uncharacteristic thoroughness that would have made Corey laugh.

I sat one last time in the upstairs hall where he died and, as in the past, tried to imagine what he might have seen in his last moments. I like to think that he chose to fix his eye on an image to take with him as he went from this place to the next. If so, his eye might easily have caught the black-and-white photo just outside his office of our boys, then four and seven, dressed as pirates, eyes glaring at the photographer as if to say: *Come at us with everything you have. We're ready.*

Of course they were just playing at it then.

I hope Corey was able to take that image with him. As much as I am keeping, I like to think he kept something, too.

I finished. Wiped the pared fingernails from the bathroom sink and silvery hairs from the shower. Rinsed a few errant parsley leaves from the vegetable crisper. Packed the handful of items I'd somehow missed: a flyswatter, hangers, socks.

I brought them back to our home, full to bursting with what was left of my ex-husband.

It has been a heartbreak and an honor to be Corey's "one," to have been, despite the failure of our marriage, the most important person in his life.

Yes, we were heading into our separate futures. Yes, he had a girlfriend who would probably have met the boys in due time. Yet in the end I was the one who went to sweep the corners clean, to save what was precious, and to close the door on his life. Don't we all hope that when our time comes, we will have one such person left who will know what to do and feel privileged to do it?

Ten months after Corey's death, the boys are moving on admirably with their lives, having perhaps inherited their father's levelheadedness in such matters. And I have kept the promise I made to Corey back when we both thought he would live long enough to become infirm: I have brought him home.

Jennifer Just lives in Woodbridge, Connecticut. She is currently writing a book about her great-great-grandfather, George B. Swift, who became mayor of Chicago in 1893 after an assassination, two fistfights, and three votes. This essay appeared in June 2005.

THE THIRD HALF OF A COUPLE

HOWIE KAHN

I T'S A BIG MORNING FOR ME: A BREAKFAST DATE at my place, and I'm cooking. I've scoured the markets and rounded up the best of everything: oranges for zesting, pears for roasting, balsamic for drizzling, goat cheese for crumbling, and, to amp up my French toast, a vial of organic Mexican vanilla beans for eviscerating and flecking. I've even grated the cinnamon myself. That's just what you do when someone special is coming over.

After completing my knife work, I set the table (folding the napkins into caterer's shapes), float pink peony blossoms in a glass bowl, take a quick shower, and put on a well-worn black T-shirt and a good pair of ripped jeans. At 11:00 a.m.—right on time—the buzzer sounds.

I answer the door, and there they are, my "date": eager, radiant, and, most appealingly, married.

I know this setup sounds potentially kinky, but there's

no sexual dynamic to report on here. No threesome will commence once the fruit is caramelized. My guests, Cory and Jake, are faithful to each other, and I'm not looking to mess that up. On the contrary, I depend on the stability of their marriage; I need them to stay together so I can go where they go and do what they do. Simply put, I'm their third wheel.

With them it's a role I was conscripted to from the start. When I moved to New York (for graduate school), Cory, my friend from college, already lived there and, luckily, had a spare bedroom. I promptly rented it and soon met Jake, her new boyfriend.

Since he was on hiatus from his work in finance, and I had class only twice a week, we spent a lot of time together, mostly tossing around balls of various dimensions.

About a month before Jake proposed to Cory, he came into my room—the one right next to Cory's—and held out a small lacquered box.

"Hey," he said casually, "can you hold onto this for me?"

I looked at his offering and gulped. My eyes misted over.

Proudly Jake gave me permission to open it, and carefully I did: the ring was glimmering, perfect, surprisingly tall.

"I don't want Cory to find it," he said. "So if you'll take it for now, I'm giving it to you."

"Yes," I whispered and deposited the diamond into my drawer on top of my graphing calculator.

Soon after, Jake took Cory to a farm in Pennsylvania to propose, and like me before her, she accepted. When they returned from their Dominican honeymoon, it became evident that married life fit us all handsomely. Their needs were fulfilled by each other; my needs were fulfilled, in tandem, by them.

By then they had a home of their own but always had food and a seat for me at their table (this at a time when I owned no furniture and bought very few groceries). Cory invited me over to talk about books and movies. Jake brought me along to play pickup basketball with his friends. Cory and I attended theater and museums. Jake and I went to a Rangers game and watched the World Series. Cory counseled me on what I fondly referred to as the ever-widening gap between me and every woman on the planet. Jake weighed in on that one, too.

We had a good thing going, a completely heartening domestic routine. Our dinners and talks took up entire nights. Cory would often fall asleep in the middle of the conversation, and I'd exit quietly, feeling satisfied, loved.

It didn't take long for me to stop dating entirely. It seemed pointless, since I already had a part in a very solid marriage.

I'd always coveted this sort of steadiness, always aspired to have my own share of it. But it's never been easy. I'm no lothario, after all, and I've long felt cut off from any dating ritual that doesn't include leaving behind a calling card with an overweight and overcorseted aunt.

I'm anachronistic, more at ease pursuing one emotionally intimate moment than braiding bodies for hours on end with some smoky-haired stranger. That and the rigors of dating have simply pushed me to unhealthy extremes—even to the hospital.

A few summers back, I endured a bout of chronic stomach pain. At the time the thing had its own seismic agenda:

rumbling, simmering, gurgling, even spurting little smoldering bits of itself up into the back of my throat. This was my body's response to a brilliantly sassy but ultimately unreachable woman for whom, at the time, I lived and breathed.

In the examining room a doctor pressed his fingers into my midsection and probed my chest with his stethoscope. "Heart sounds fine," he said. "Very strong."

I wasn't surprised. Women don't begin to do damage to my heart until they've utterly ripped apart my stomach. I told him this. He nodded sympathetically, then sent me packing with a prescription for a bowel relaxer.

Post-hospitalization, I began seeing other women. But the result, sadly, was a brand-new set of pseudo-gastroenterological dilemmas, which made me late, loopy, or a little green when I arrived for a date. As I was getting ready, my stomach would churn until it felt as if it were on the verge of popping out a stick of butter. It would take at least twenty-five minutes for my discomfort to pass naturally. Or fifteen minutes and a Xanax. Or five minutes and a finger down the throat.

Cory and Jake proved to be my panacea, better than all the other remedies (Tums, psychotherapy, Julie Delpy in *Before Sunrise*) that made love seem to me, momentarily, like a thing without fangs. So I got close to them, clung to them fiercely. It felt almost as if I were following a biological directive, the one that permits little creatures to seek protection and nourishment by piggybacking on the hide of a much larger animal.

Some of what we did as a threesome, although my participation was de rigueur and always welcome, I probably should have let them do alone, as a couple. Like dimly lighted birthday dinners at which Cory looked like a bigamist sand-wiched between Jake and me, or the trip to the Bronx Zoo, where we all shared ice cream cones and, at my urging, rode the Skyfari cable car four times.

At one point I noticed a few baboons cavorting on a grassy slope below: three of them tumbling down the hill. At the bottom, though, a pair of them, holding hands, started climbing back toward the top while the third strutted off alone.

Primates weren't the only ones sending me signals. Cory and Jake now had a message for me, too. I don't remember exactly how they said it. Did they announce over dinner that they were leaving me for another city? Or break the news under a streetlamp just as it started to rain? Or send carnations with a note? I have no idea.

Whatever the case, their explanation that they were moving from New York to Portland (Oregon! Not even Maine!) slid, as if lubricated by its absurdity, in one ear and out the other. Having been blissfully sheltered for so long by the elemental passivity of third-wheeldom, I didn't hear them, or couldn't, because I was no longer fluent in the lan-guage of breakups and relationship anxiety.

Leaving? Moving? Goodbye? The words all sounded tan-gled and distant, as if from an Urdu phrase book or a Kelly Clarkson song.

The night Cory and Jake left, I cried so hard that I hyperventilated for the first time in my life. Without a paper bag in sight, I stuffed an unlaundered hand towel into my mouth like a horse's bit and huffed out what felt like the holdings of my entire pulmonary cavity.

When I finally caught my breath and extracted the towel

(it left gauzy strands of lint on my tongue and between several of my teeth), I was shivering on my bathroom floor, knees tucked up against my chest. Out loud I said, "What the hell is wrong with me? People leave all the time. Deal with it."

But I couldn't deal with it, so I called my dad. "What's wrong with me?" I asked him.

"It's hard," he said, "to have your safety net yanked out from under you. It hurts."

At this point—it was 2:30 a.m.—I slid a couple of melatonin discs under my tongue.

Dad paused. "Being on your own for a while—it's probably going to be good for you."

Next thing I knew the sun had come up, and my face was half frozen, striated from the air-conditioner I'd used as a pillow.

I always knew that going through a divorce would crush me, send me over the edge, induce beard growth and religious indoctrination and spectral dreaming. But I'd never said any vows of my own, so I couldn't let things get that far out of hand. Besides, I could still fight this, couldn't I? I could move to Portland, too.

I really thought about it: about leaving New York and incorporating granola into my diet. I'd learn to recycle, strap on the Gore-Tex, and spend weekends tromping around sub-alpine berry patches. In Oregon I could preserve my date-free, risk-free reality.

But that would be pathetic, cowardly. Even the baboon at the zoo was able to walk away, and he's supposed to be my evolutionary inferior.

I started focusing on my convalescence. Rilke and Grey

Goose and Häagen-Dazs mango ice cream each played pivotal roles. But the real defibrillatory jolt came from what I now consider to be an alternative source of healing: online dating (Cory's idea).

I didn't go on any dates right away, but the shock of getting so much attention from strangers based solely on my posted photograph lifted my spirits considerably. I even started believing that some special girl out there just might have something more sublime to offer me than the usual ulcer. This sudden surge of faith wasn't exactly matrimonial bliss, but it felt like progress, an opportunity to get back in the game.

I *would* rebound, I realized, and that deserved a reward. So I decided to take a little trip. To Portland, of course.

Howie Kahn is a contributing editor for WSJ: The Wall Street Journal Magazine, *co-author of the* New York Times *bestseller* Sneakers, *author of* Becoming a Private Investigator, *and host of* Prince Street, *a food and culture podcast heard in more than two hundred countries. This essay appeared in October 2005.*

WHEN I WAS SIXTEEN, I PLACED HIM FOR ADOPTION. COULD WE TRY AGAIN?

MEREDITH HALL

THE CALL CAME IN MAY.

"Hello," the woman said. "My name is Ann Hurd. I work with the New Hampshire courts. I want you to sit down. Your son is looking for you."

I had been hoping for this call for twenty-one years, and it came like a dream into an ordinary spring day.

"We will take this very slowly," she said. "This can cause enormous problems for both the child and the birth mother."

"But I'm ready now. I've been waiting for years."

"First you will write letters for a while, through me. It is devastating to the child to experience a second abandonment."

"I could never abandon him again."

"But it happens a lot," she said.

"Where is he?"

"I can't tell you that yet."

"Can you tell me his name?" I felt myself separate from my voice.

"His name," she said, "is Ron."

This sound was electric. My son had a name!

"Your son," Ann told me, "is extraordinary. Ron is a spectacular young man."

Three weeks later, a letter finally came through Ann. There was a picture enclosed, my first sight of my lost child. It was blurred and gray, but here was Ron—serious, a strong jaw, intelligent eyes.

Dear Meredith, he wrote. *I don't know what to say. I don't know how to do this. Ron.*

His handwriting was slanted along the page, hurried. I carried his note in my pocket, reading it again and again as I stared at his photograph.

Ann called and said, "Write back to him right away. He is very scared. Ask him some questions."

Dear Ron. My name is Meredith Hall. I live in East Booth-bay on the coast of Maine. I have a son, Morgan, who is 10. And a son named Zachary, who is 7. We keep sheep and chickens and big gardens. Tell me about your family. Tell me about your room. Tell me about what you like to do. I want you to know that I have always loved you.

Ann edited our letters for revealing details. They came to us blacked out:

My name is Meredith——. I live in——on the coast of——.

My name is Ron——. I grew up on a farm in——in

southern——. My mother and father,——and——, are very loving and supportive.

Our ghost lives slowly took shape. Five months later, Ann arranged for us to meet.

It was 10:00 a.m., October 18. Ron drove slowly along my dirt road. He glanced at me quickly as I stood waiting on the porch steps. I could see blond hair, curls. He turned off the engine, got out of the car, looked at me, and our eyes locked. He was thin, athletic, handsome. My son. He was not a child. He was a young man, wearing jeans, a striped sweater, and soft old loafers. He came toward me, his shoes crunching on the stone path. His teeth were brilliant white, with a space in the front. My father had a space like that. I moved toward him. Every day, for twenty-one years, I had played this scene. I had never known what to do, and I did not know now. I was breaking with joy, and with grief, too, because here he was a grown man, here I was nearly forty— all those years lost forever. I reached for him, held him to me, a stranger, my son, this beautiful, radiant, terrified, smiling son.

We did not hold each other long because we were shy, strangers to each other. We walked to the railing of the porch and stood, three feet between us, facing the river, looking out over the coast of Maine. I could not find the question that would start our life together. What I wanted to ask was, Have you felt my love each day? Have you felt me missing you? Have you known how sorry I am? Have you been loved? Have you been happy? Will you forgive me?

All I could come up with was "Do you like UNH?"

"Yes." His first word to me. His voice was soft and deep.

"What year are you?"

"Well, I'm working my way through so I have another two years."

His body was taut, as if he were ready to fight something off. His face was open, his eyes enormous, blue, set wide apart. He had a scar across his chin. He was very serious. He turned to me and smiled suddenly. He had deep dimples. My brother had those dimples. We smiled, then turned to the ocean again in overwhelmed silence.

"Do you want to go for a walk?" I asked. I felt deep happiness, which stirred old sorrow into wild confusion.

We walked down the dirt road to the river, blurting out every thought that came, our conversation leaping as we tried to reconstruct the lost years.

"This is the owl tree," I said. "Morgan and Zachary are my sons. Your brothers." I saw Ron tense for just a moment, then slip back into the rhythm of our walking. "They find owl pellets here and we dissect them."

Ron said, "My mother let me play hooky to go fishing with her."

My mother. I breathed. Of course. We were two mothers.

We sat on an old bench above the undulating seaweed, talking fast. I knew he would drive away that afternoon, and I didn't know if he would ever come again. He must have wondered if I would want him to come again. Sometimes, we found ourselves laughing. Twice, Ron said, "I've never told anyone this before."

We climbed back up the hill, and I showed him the downstairs of our homey little Cape.

"Do you want to see your brothers' rooms?" I asked.

"Yes," he said quietly.

He glanced quickly into their sunny rooms, at their toys and books, at his brothers' lives here with me, where they've been loved, safe, not given away. We went back down to the kitchen. Eating tuna sandwiches, we returned to our stories, the joy we felt right at that minute lying like a pond within our grief.

"Would you like me to tell you about your father?"

His hands stopped midair, a picture of our first day I will never forget, the image of his powerful hunger to belong.

"You look like him," I said. "I was sixteen, and he was a sophomore in college. We met at the beach. He came to see me after you were born, for five or six years, showing up, never asking any questions."

I watched him struggle to integrate this information into his twenty-one-year-old identity.

"It doesn't matter anyway" was all he could say.

He let me hug him goodbye at his car. He called on Wednesday and said he was coming on Sunday.

"Can the boys be there?" he asked.

I was overcome by his courage. It was the beginning of our new family.

I ached with guilt about my two young sons, understanding that I was asking them to take in stride the effects of my own enormous history. They never balked. When I told them they had a big brother, they immediately embraced him. They stood in front of Ron at that first meeting and grinned. They climbed on him, giggling. Like monkeys, they studied every inch of him, probing and touching, pulling off his socks and shoes, studying his toes and hands and back, comparing them with their own. They peered inside his mouth. Morgan draped his arm over Ron's shoulder while they sat on the couch; Zachary got in under Ron's arm. Ron came every Sunday, then for weekends, then for the summer. I was stunned by my sons' capacity to include him, to give him part of me.

And Ron took me to his family, too. "This is my mother, Rose," he said. "This is my other mother, Meredith." He did not call me Mom, or Mum, or Mumma, like Morgan and Zachary. He had a mother. He had a sister, Tammy, adopted when she was two. He had a father, Hank. Astonishingly, Rose and Hank welcomed me as if they were happy I had come into Ron's life. I felt as if I had stolen their son.

Those months were confusing, upheaving, yet laughter often filled the house. And we cried. We rested in our deep love for each other, then we would fly apart in despair or hurt. Some days we needed to be reassured that this was forever. Other days, we fought for our lives, the lives that had worked pretty well before. Sometimes we couldn't contain everything that had been lost.

I had never told my friends about this child. The grief and shame of losing him at sixteen had stayed with me all my life as a fiercely private sorrow. Now they argued with me, telling me that Morgan and Zachary should not have to pay the price of my history. "Are you telling me I should send this child away again?" I asked. Yes, they said. This isn't fair to your children. But an older friend disagreed, telling me, "This is your son. Don't listen to them. This is a miracle. It is a fairy tale with a happy ending."

Then it was October 18 again, our first anniversary. Our days had found rhythm. The upheaving emotions were quieting. My friend was right: this was a miracle, a fairy tale, though each day felt fragile, as if it all might disappear if we turned our backs. Still, our old lives receded, and our new family held together. I had my son. He had his mother.

To mark the day, I gave him my small clay owl, the only thing I had from those devastated years after he was born. "This is to remind you every day that this place in my life is forever," I said.

He gave me an acorn. "My renaissance," he said, his voice soft and hopeful.

There were no patterns for how to do this, how to hold each other safely and fully after a lifetime apart. We could not plot out the future. We were a family. We loved each other. We needed each other. That was our only map.

Meredith Hall lives on the coast of Maine; her first novel, Here, will be published in the fall of 2019. This essay appeared in March 2005.

WHEN THE DOORMAN IS YOUR MAIN MAN

JULIE MARGARET HOGBEN

IT WAS SUMMERTIME IN MANHATTAN, DARK AND balmy, almost midnight, on the Upper West Side. He and I rounded the corner from Amsterdam. Drinks had gone well. Walking me home, he held my hand. Tipsy, I said, "You can't come up," and stopped near a stoop.

"I don't want to," he said coyly, placing his hands on my waist, drawing me close. "But I do want to see you again." He smiled.

I smiled. "What I mean is, if you want to kiss me good night, it has to be here." We weren't even close to my building.

"But I thought you lived in"—he said, craning his neck to look for street signs—"the Nineties?"

"I do." I started to stammer, to try to explain. "I do, but see, he knows we're on our first date, and there's a window he can see out of onto the sidewalk, and sometimes he's waiting. If I'm too late, he can get worried."

"Who?" my date asked, looking concerned. "Who can see us?"

"Um," I hedged.

"Your boyfriend?"

"No."

"Your dad?"

"No, no. It's hard to—"

"Your husband? You're married?"

I sighed and shrugged, flying my freak flag, ruining the moment. I took a deep breath. "My doorman."

Guzim was my doorman, and ours was a common and unsung friendship, that between women living in New York, single and alone, and the doormen who take care of them, acting as gatekeepers, bodyguards, confidants, and father figures; the doormen who protect and deliver much more than Zappos boxes and FreshDirect, not because it's part of the job, but because they're good men.

"I don't like him," Guzim said of a new guy I was dating two months later. He whispered this over the intercom.

I entered the lobby and saw them outside, my doorman and my date on the sidewalk, laughing and chatting. My date turned to flick his cigarette away, and Guzim took the moment to shoot me a look: He had gotten the scoop and was already wary.

I waved goodbye as my date and I walked off. When I glanced back, Guzim shook his head. I rolled my eyes. What did he know? What could he tell from a ten-minute talk?

My date turned out to be sexy and funny, spoke gorgeous Hebrew, and partied too much. And so I agreed to a second drink and saw him again, and again, as autumn drew on. I was always attracted to bad boys.

Guzim wasn't a bad boy. He was kind and well man-
nered, a gray-haired cross between Cary Grant and George
Clooney. Born in Albania in the mid-1940s, he hailed from
an educated military family; his father had been an army
general. When Guzim was nineteen, the communist leader
Enver Hoxha's secret police arrested and interned his family, accusing them of treason.

For twenty years, he lived in a labor camp, forced to
farm in a remote area, not unlike Stalin's gulags. "My whole
life as a young man," he said to me once. He never married.
Never had children.

At thirty-nine, he was finally released, and the United
States granted his family asylum. He found a job as a white-
glove doorman in New York. Whenever I asked him how he
was, on any day, at any hour, he always said, "No complaints."

This was his mantra.

On Halloween night that same year, I walked home
again, this time alone, from the twenty-four-hour CVS. I
couldn't sleep. In pajama bottoms, T-shirt, and Uggs, I skipped
up the steps into the lobby, a white paper bag clenched in
my hand.

Hidden inside was a pregnancy test.

Guzim was resting on his usual stool, half-on, half-off,
and looked up from his *New York Post*. "What?" he said.

"What?" I said. "Nothing."

"What is it?"

"Nothing." I sailed past and held up the bag. "Headache.
Tylenol."

"No," he said in a drawn-out way, shaking his head, folding his newspaper closed.

I couldn't fool him.

I stopped and looked around. No one was in the lobby. Fine. It was well after midnight, so I doubled back. "I think, I don't know—" I bit my lip. "I missed a, you know." My face contorted, and I started to cry.

Guzim waited, then said, "The Israeli?"

"Yes! And I don't even like him," I said, wiping my tears. "He's a liar. I can't spend the rest of my life with him."

"So don't," Guzim said, straightening the cuffs of his uniform jacket. We stood and talked for two more hours.

I was distraught. I thought I had been safe, counted the days and done the math, used protection—most of the time. "How did this happen?" I stupidly asked.

"How?" Guzim said with a wry smile. "Come on. It's life."

Two weeks later, I told the father. He seemed at once delighted and horrified. A few weeks later, he even proposed.

I politely declined. He didn't want to be a parent. Not really. We didn't want to marry each other. We both knew the truth.

I said I'd raise the baby myself, and he could be involved as little or as much as he wanted to be. He was off the hook, as long as we kept the drama at bay and stayed in touch. We three would be friends, if not family. He agreed.

Three months later and starting to show, I broke the news to everyone else. My Catholic parents, married over forty years, feared for my future as a single mother. I didn't blame them. My girlfriends—married and single, mothers or childless—were mostly supportive.

But I became fodder for gossip: Who was the father? Did

I dump him, or did he dump me? Valid questions, some-times asked to my face, sometimes not.

But down in the lobby, Guzim was there with no dog in the race. I wasn't his daughter, sister, or ex. I wasn't his em-ployee or boss. Our social circles didn't overlap. Six days a week, he stood downstairs, detached but also caring enough to be the perfect friend, neither worried nor pitying.

It was he who signed for the crib when it came, for the onesies, bottles, and boxes of diapers. It was he who asked how I felt every day. I saw the Israeli every few weeks.

Guzim and I talked a lot over those nine months, and his worldly perspective comforted me: more European than tri-state, more Cold War than twenty-first century, and grounded in gratitude.

His stance was resolute. He upheld and honored me for my choice, and protected my dignity and self-esteem. I was still young, he reminded me. I could still meet a man and get married. I had a master's degree, a job, savings.

So what if I wasn't married? Look at the world. Worse things had happened in history. Please. We would be fine. My baby was a gift.

In August, while I was away for the weekend, my water broke early, and I gave birth in Providence, Rhode Island. Two days later, my parents picked me up and drove me south on Route 95 to the Upper West Side and home.

When my father pulled up, Guzim knew the car. He skipped down the steps and swung the back door open wide. Somehow he knew what was waiting inside.

I climbed out, exhausted and teary. We hugged. I turned back, unclipped the car seat and pulled it out. We both gazed at the sleeping newborn, impossibly pretty.

"Beautiful," he said. "Wonderful job."

Nine days later, the Israeli left for good. His father was sick back home, he said. But we were friends and on good terms, and for the next year, I emailed him photos. He called and we laughed as he kept me awake during those first long, sleepless months.

But Guzim's was the face we saw every day, the man who said good morning and good night to my girl, who smiled and cooed and remarked on her growth, her smile, and her first words.

The Israeli kept in touch for over a year and then disappeared. No more emails or calls. I'd send photos, and he'd send silence.

My daughter held a special affection for Guzim, almost as if she understood the role he had played as someone who welcomed her into this world with open arms, an open heart, ready and willing to guard and protect her, just as he had guarded and protected her mother.

Once she could, she'd run down the sidewalk, arms outstretched, and he'd catch her up into a big hug.

Her father doesn't call or visit, and we don't call or visit him. But we visit Guzim.

We live in California now, but when we're in New York, we drop by the building, hoping to find Guzim at his post. Sometimes he is. Sometimes he isn't. But we always check.

And when we find him and he asks how I'm doing, I look at my girl and say, "No complaints."

Julie Margaret Hogben is a teacher and a mother to one little girl. She lives in Los Angeles and is still single. This essay appeared in October 2015.

PERMISSIONS